created for so much more

SOARING WITH GOD

DEBORAH GALL

DEDICATION

To my husband, Rick, with all my love.

After 40 wonderful years, I know there is still *so much more*—I can't wait!

"And I will give them one heart and one way, that they may fear Me always, for their own good and for the good of their children after them" (Jeremiah 32:39).

Selah Press PUBLISHING

Created For So Much More: Soaring With God

Copyright © 2017, by Deborah Gall

ISBN-13: 978-0692889718 (Selah Press)
ISBN-10: 069288971X

Printed in The United States of America
Published by Selah Press, LLC, selah-press.com
Editor, Loral Pepoon, cowriterpro.com
Cover Art: © 2017, by Deborah Gall
Cover Design: Victoria R Carlson | Design, victoria-carlson.squarespace.com

Style: Editorial liberties have been taken for emphasis. Names of God and references to Him are capitalized, and satan and the enemy are lowercased.

CONTENTS

FOREWORD

Dear Readers,

I have had the privilege of attending Deborah's conferences as well as having times of personal ministry with her. Each time, I left with a greater sense of how much God loves me and who He created me to be.

God has used Deborah's teaching and exercises to break my paralyzing fear of repeating past relational mistakes. The dissipation of this fear enabled me to more fully embrace the freedom of my transformed life, which God had radically changed less than a year before I met Deborah. God's outpouring of love also smashed the lie of unworthiness that I still felt—despite His deliverance from consequences of past mistakes. Shortly after I attended my first conference with Deborah, I met the man that God had chosen for me, and we were married within several months. As a couple, we continue to attend Deborah's conferences and apply the material, and our marriage becomes stronger, gripped in Christ's love.

In early September 2016, I couldn't stop thinking about Deborah's material and how God has used it to impact my life. My husband and I have benefitted from it, but I also wanted others to experience it. I thought, "God, this life-changing material needs to be available to anyone, at any time! I would be so honored to help get Deborah's book edited and published!"

A few days later, I reached out to Deborah, who had previously mentioned that she was working on writing the conference material in book form. God's timing was perfect! He had just confirmed to her that, after a season away from the manuscript, it was time to get back to work and to publish the book.

Nine months after God's promptings to both of us, *Created For So Much More* was born!

As a book editor, I do not often write the foreword for a book, but as a person who has personally been changed by the material contained within this book, I accepted Deborah's invitation to introduce these 12 testimonies and the chapters beyond.

I attest to the power to change lives that runs through this material. I pray that these stories spur you on to discover how God has created you for *so much more,* and I hope that they inspire you to accept God's invitation to soar with Him!

In Christ,
Loral Pepoon, Editor, *Created For So Much More*

TESTIMONIES

"As a newlywed in a second marriage, I asked God during the Cloud Forming exercise about being a Christ-like husband. He showed me that I needed to support my wife's writing pursuits. She was invited to a 30-day blog challenge just days later. As I participated with her, **God uncovered my writing talent** that I never knew was there! Now we are writing our books and blogs together."—Seth

"I was a broken vessel the first time I heard Deborah speak, 'We are created for so much more.' **God used her words to plant seeds of hope, grace, and healing** as He showed me that He uses times of brokenness for His purpose if we let Him."—Danyalle

"I had never thought about a connection with God being anything other than an accessory in my life. **God revealed that He wants a relationship with me,** and He showed me that His spiritual language is all around me. I just needed to take the time to listen and learn His language."—Anonymous

"God works through all of Deborah's teaching to reveal the transformative power of God's truth and love. In an exercise asking about how God loves me, **I encountered His intimacy** in a profoundly deep way. **I was set free from ongoing shaming self-talk** because of guilt from my past, and then I was open to meet and accept the love of my future husband."—Loral

"I attended a *Created For So Much More* conference at a time of transition in my life. Although I wasn't certain of my new direction, **God brought confirmation** that the new path was His will. I learned to tune in to the Audience of One and continue to live listening only to Him for all aspects of my life."—Melinda

"Deborah inspires you to go deeper and higher into your destiny as you ask yourself, 'What was I created for and who does God say that I am?' God walks into every one of Deborah's conferences that I attend and **changes the atmosphere.** My life has forever changed through her ministry."—Beth

"Deborah has helped me see that God has *so much more* for me. He has sharpened my flight plan as Deborah provided a safe place to practice take-offs and landings with the Holy Spirit. Father God, Jesus, and **Holy Spirit lavishly poured out the *so much more*** that They are and what They have for each person. I will never forget the gold dust that was on Deborah's skirt and on others' hands and faces."—Lisa

"I sat at the feet of Jesus, took a deep breath, and listened to God's voice through Deborah's teaching and guided exercises. I heard God tell me to serve locally and work out my God-given dream one step at a time. One year later, **I see my big audacious dream becoming a reality** as we prepare to open So Big Mountain House Maternity Home."—Lori

"During the conference, God created a greater sense of stillness within me and showed me that I could **trust His timing**. I learned to submit to His will, and one year later, I continue to live resting in His timing."—Lisa Marie

"God gave me new revelation in my prayer life as He showed me that everything we experience on Earth has already been worked out in the Heavenly realm. I have **gained new peace and greater spiritual authority** as I have changed from praying 'Please, Lord' to declaring 'Thy will be done on Earth as it is in Heaven.' "—Lynn

"**God broadened my horizons** to see all that He has for me. He showed me that it was His strategy for me to plan and set deadlines for my goals. I continue to do this as He uses my goals, steps, and deadlines to unlock the future He has for me. I left the conference encouraged to pursue the *so much more* that the Lord had shown me in my spirit."—Vertie

"**God gave me new freedom in my creativity**. I gained trust in His timing and left with a sense of comfort and peace knowing my artistic journey was mine alone. I have faith that God will complete the details in His timing. My job is to be still, follow where He leads, and soar with Him."—Zelena

INTRODUCTION

How would you like to soar with God into the future and purpose that He has for you? It is truly possible. An amazing future—a future ripe with opportunity and overflowing with promise—lies before you. When you tune your ears to Heaven and willingly go where God leads, you soar with God to discover the *so much more* that He has for you. It doesn't matter who you are, where you've been, what you do, or where you live, God has even more for you to discover about who He created you to be and what He created you to do. Greater purpose, freedom, clarity, peace, vision and *so much more* await you as you unlock the treasures that you will find along the flight path of this God-created journey—tailor-made for you!

Whether you are new to your walk with God or you have been walking with Him for decades, you will gain more revelation and understanding of your identity and purpose through the 12 inspired lessons in this book. Each lesson presents a step in your journey with tried-and-true exercises that empower you to apply the presented truths to your personal walk with the Lord. The material and the exercises have been shared with hundreds of conference attendees who report the journey to be life-changing.

You will learn to clear out the clutter (of the enemy) so you can hear air traffic control (God's voice). God will then confirm His flight plan for you, further develop your timetable, and even teach you to enjoy the layovers and times of rest. The results will surprise and enthrall you as God—with your cooperation—unlocks your amazing future and changes the atmosphere around you! Wow!

How do you start? Simply sit down with this book, grab some coffee, your journal, and a Bible, and embark on the most exciting adventure you can imagine—the one God created just for you. Soar with Him and let your journey begin!

1.
Created For So Much More
PURPOSE:
Affecting Change

Sally's life changed forever at a *Created For So Much More* conference when Holy Spirit connected who He had created her to be with where He had placed her in the marketplace. Before the conference, even though she had walked closely with the Lord for decades, Sally had not yet uncovered the God-designed overlap of her work and her God-given purpose. God showed her that intersection—the *so much more* for her work life—was to impact the lives of people she encountered at work and to influence her work environment on His behalf. As coordinator of hospital volunteers at an esteemed hospital, she regularly interacted with hundreds of people. In an aha moment of specific instruction, God revealed that she was placed in her position not only to schedule the volunteers' time but also to build relationships with them. She suddenly saw these connection points as opportunities for her to open her heart and let the Holy Spirit work through her to minister to their needs. She left the conference excited and equipped to apply her God-given purpose to affect change in her world of work.

The more I have taught this material, the more I realize how many believers are like Sally, simply because they haven't actively and regularly sought the connection between their current situation and their God-given purpose. Many brothers and sisters in Christ understand that they are God-created unique individuals, yet they stumble over the understanding that He designed them for a specific Kingdom purpose. In fact, we all have a Kingdom purpose to affect change in the world. That change begins to happen when you recognize who God created you to be and what He created you to do, AND it continues as you live a life that reflects your God-given identity, fully engaged in your God-given purpose. When you live authentically and purposefully, you soar with God to change the world around you.

Created For a Purpose

Our God created the world intentionally, with beauty and purpose. When we look at sunsets and the stars, we can see, as David did: *"The heavens are telling of the glory of God; And their expanse is declaring the work of His hands"* (Psalm 19:1). God has infused purpose in everything—from the smallest gnats to every person—including you. Your purpose is to fill a need that only you can address. God—who is all-knowing—recognized a need in the world first, and then He created you with your purpose in mind. He blended just the right elements in you—like gifting, leanings, personality, and looks—that are required to fulfill your purpose.

Like a master chef, God selected the perfect set of ingredients to make the perfect dish that is you. Any good chef knows the purpose of a dish BEFORE he creates it. Many criteria must be considered to accomplish the ultimate goal for a chef's masterpiece. He needs to consider the season, the time of day the dish will be served, and understand how the dish will fulfill the greater vision for the meal. Every ingredient is chosen for a specific reason to achieve a particular purpose. You are no different. Scripture tells us that God had your purpose in mind when He created you.

> *For You formed my inward parts;*
> *You wove me in my mother's womb.*
> *I will give thanks to You, for I am fearfully and wonderfully made;*
> *Wonderful are Your works,*
> *And my soul knows it very well.*
> *My frame was not hidden from you,*
> *When I was made in secret,*
> *And skillfully wrought in the depths of the earth;*
> *Your eyes have seen my unformed substance;*
> *And in Your book were all written*
> *The days that were ordained for me,*
> *When as yet there was not one of them* (Psalm 139:13–16).

> *"Before I formed you in the womb I knew you,*
> *And before you were born I consecrated you"* (Jeremiah 1:5).

You, like the Psalmist, were created with ordered days *"when as yet there was not one of them"* (Psalm 139:16). You, like Jeremiah, were set apart for a specific purpose before you were formed in your mother's womb. God combined the precise amount of gifts, talents, personality, and physical characteristics that you possess. He then placed you in your exact family and brought you into the world at a precise time because He needed you exactly where you are at this moment.

You may be asking yourself how God could have a purpose for your life when just getting through the day is a challenge. Perhaps you live with a spouse who is more dictator than partner. For some, a childhood full of fear and pain has caused rifts of the soul that never seem to mend. Poverty may have caused you to make choices of which you are ashamed. Do I understand the reason for the abuse, terror, or devastating conditions with which some of God's children must live? Not at all. I will never understand. The truth is we aren't entitled to understand. What we know and trust is that God is sovereign and His ways are often beyond our understanding.

"For My thoughts are not your thoughts,
Nor are your ways My ways," declares the Lord.
"For as the heavens are higher than the earth,
So are My ways higher than your ways
And My thoughts than your thoughts" (Isaiah 55:8–9).

Living life as a Jesus Follower means trusting God with the "why" of life's occurrences and pursuing His plan and purpose for your life, in spite of how your circumstances look or how you feel on any given day. Whatever your situation, God has a reason, purpose, and destiny—also known as a plan—for your life. Believing this truth is where faith comes in, Dear One. Trust that the Lord is who He says He is. He created you for His plan and purpose, and as the Apostle Paul tells us in Romans, *"God causes all things to work together for good to those who love God, to those who are called according to His purpose"* (Romans 8:28). **You are called according to His purpose. If you love Him, He promises to work all things together for your good.**

The good news is that we don't have to understand the "why" of life. We live in the knowledge of and have faith in His promise to be faithful to our purpose. As Paul wrote to the Thessalonians, *"Faithful is He who calls you, and He also will bring it to pass"* (1 Thessalonians 5:24).

I have an uncle who is 95 years old. Four years ago, his body was literally starving itself. He could no longer process protein, the building block of life. He was completely bedridden and required nearly around-the-clock professional care. One day, his body began to heal. Suddenly, his protein levels began to rise. Today, I am happy to report that he lives a vibrant life at his retirement community. A couple of years ago, he asked if he still had a purpose. My response was, "Absolutely!" In that moment, he said, "I think I'm supposed to write my memoirs." I don't understand why my uncle had to go through that pain and suffering. I do know that on the other side of it, he lives with a greater sense of purpose than ever. After he told me about his thoughts about his memoirs, he dedicated himself to writing his story as if it was a regular job. At my last visit, his memoirs were complete and being edited for publication. Purpose is not constrained by age, profession, location, or education. If you are living and breathing on Earth, you have purpose.

You may have found yourself asking the Lord to reveal your purpose in life when you ask, "Why am I here?" That question is, in essence, what my uncle was asking. It is a question that is foundational to the journey on which we embark. For the sake of our journey, let's expand the question a bit and ask, "For what purpose was I created in this time and place, with these unique qualities, gifts, talents, and with this personality?" That question should tug at every believer's heart and spirit because God created every person to search, find, and fulfill the answer to that question. He beckons you to live purposefully as the unique person He created you to be.

Created to Change the World

You were formed within a framework of personality, occupation, gender, and location to influence, affect, and change the world in which you live. That, my friend, is your Kingdom purpose in a nutshell. Let me say that again: God created you to affect change in the world in which you live. The canvas of your life fits perfectly within the framework of who God created you to be. The life that is reflected on your canvas has the power to change the world in the same way one of my paintings changed a woman's life.

Several years ago, I received a phone call from a client who told me how God used one of my paintings to touch his mother. She had felt poorly enough to make an appointment with her doctor, and was on her way to the appointment, when she stopped at her son's house. Her son was busy when she got there, so she went into his living room to sit and wait for him. While she sat, she was captivated by his new painting—the one I had painted for him. After several minutes passed, she stood up, walked into the kitchen where her son was, and made a phone call. When her son asked who she had called, she replied, "The doctor's office. I was sitting in your living room, looking at that new painting, and suddenly I feel better. I don't need to see the doctor anymore."

Jehovah Rapha, the Lord who heals, had touched that woman's

physical body as she engaged with that painting! That piece of artwork symbolized God's Presence pouring from Heaven to Earth. It was created in an atmosphere of worship in the Presence of God.

The truth is that any art, created from a place of worship, a place of abiding in the Presence of God, or a place of encountering God, sets a transaction in motion in the spiritual realm that we cannot even begin to comprehend. You could say that these works of art become heart-to-heart gateways that have the power to affect change in people's lives. I share that story as an example of how anything created from an encounter with God can serve as a means for others to encounter God.

Living Gateways

Here's what I really want you to grab hold of—You are God's masterpiece. You, Dear One, are no different than my painting in your ability to affect change. As YOU live from a place of worship, a place of abiding in the Presence of God—a place of encountering God, you become a gateway that has the power to affect change. You may not feel that you have the power to affect change, but God does. He sees you as a living gateway and a door of destiny.

So wake up, you living gateways!
Lift up your heads, you ageless doors of destiny!
Welcome the King of Glory, for He is about to come through you!
(Psalm 24:7 The Passion Translation, TPT).

Did you get that? You are a living gateway that opens the way for others to be transformed as they encounter the Father, Son, and Holy Spirit in you. The way that you change the world could be as varied as your life's canvas and framework. You may be a teacher, a business executive, a factory worker, a physical therapist, a receptionist, or a sales person. You may be in high school or newly-retired. Wherever you find yourself, the Lord asks you to become a living gateway by living a life focused on Heaven and fully engaged with Father, Jesus, and Holy Spirit. That revelation of being a living gateway is what Sally, the conference attendee from the beginning of the chapter, experienced. She recognized that by inviting God into her work life, He would shine through her to change others and the environment around her.

I encourage you to welcome the King of Glory into every nook and cranny of your life as you soar with God. The exercises throughout this book invite Father, Jesus, and Holy Spirit into your life in such a way that you become *so much more* aware of who God created you to be and what He created you to do. You are different than who He created anyone else to be, and He uses that different approach to fulfill His divine purpose and plan for your life.

Same Purpose, Different Approaches

Several years ago, the Lord shed light on different approaches to life when I was asked the hypothetical question: What would each of the members of my family do if a brick wall suddenly appeared in front of the path where we were walking? As I thought about this imaginary wall, I realized all four members of my household would respond differently. My older son would run straight into that wall to ensure that it was, in fact, made of brick and ascertain that it would indeed impede his progress. Only after he ran into it, would he try to climb it, knock it down, or figure out a way around it. My husband, on the other hand, would undoubtedly analyze the wall and get to work determining how to remove the obstacle that he faced. My younger son would decide that a brick wall would make a great backdrop for a comedic act, and while others figured out how to take it down, he'd begin to entertain everyone. You might have an entirely different approach.

Maybe you are more like me. At the time when I was first asked about this hypothetical brick wall, I would have started to worry about my ability to stay on schedule with this obstacle around the corner. Today, I would undoubtedly paint the wall with an arched opening, and then I would pray, believing that the Lord would make a way when there seemed to be no way. You still may not see yourself in any of these approaches—and that's actually the point. We each approach life's situations in ways that reveal our God-given mix of personality, gifts, talents, and character.

We all look at each situation and do life in unique ways. Hallelujah! Your unique approach reflects your God-given identity and a unique "who"—who God created you to be. You were also created with a "what"—your purpose. When God created you with a purpose in mind, He created you to affect change in your own specific and unique ways. Combining your "who" with your "what" enables you to find what I call the sweet spot of the *so much more* that awaits. The sweet spot is the intersection of your identity and your purpose.

How to Get Started Finding Your Purpose

Are you feeling a bit overwhelmed at the notion that God created you to affect change in the world around you? Are you a bit anxious to figure out that sweet spot of your identity and your purpose? Do you wonder how the Lord is going to show you what you need to know to change the world around you? Those questions are perfect! They tell me that you are ready to receive what the Lord has for you. They tell me that you are here for a reason. They tell me that you are here, at this moment, reading this page, because you answered the Lord's invitation to be transformed by His Spirit.

Throughout this book, we will take time to allow Holy Spirit to do His transforming work. The headings, "**SOARING WITH GOD**," indicate that at least one exercise follows. These exercises are connection points along our journey that allow you time to sit with the Lord, to ponder what you have read in this book in light of your own life, and to discover how to apply what Holy Spirit speaks. The exercises give you time and space to bask in God's Presence, inviting Him to show you the *so much more* for your life. These exercises are the same ones that I have used in my coaching appointments and at my conferences. I promise that if you submit to the process and to Holy Spirit's words and nudging, you will indeed be transformed. In fact, the exercises are favorites among conference attendees because they offer an opportunity to soar to Heaven and bring Heaven's perspective back to Earth within the context of daily life. As one attendee wrote, "I love the exercises. Through them, the information presented becomes practical and personal. They answer the questions 'What does this mean to me?' and 'How do I apply this to my life?' "

SOARING WITH GOD

For most of these exercises, I will ask you to grab a notebook, journal, blank paper, and pen or pencil. I actually recommend a three-ring binder or a spiral notebook so that you can keep all of your exercises in the same place. Trust me that you will refer to the exercises multiple times—not just during this journey—but also beyond this book as you move into the *so much more* that God has for you. Marsha, another conference attendee, told me that she used the exercises over and over again in her daily life. She said, "This notebook has become my handbook for walking with God."

In general, I will suggest that you give yourself a fair amount of time to center yourself with the Lord before actually doing an exercise. To center yourself means to be silent before Him, perhaps as soft music plays in the background. Allow time for the veil between Heaven and Earth to become translucent. Give Holy Spirit time to permeate the atmosphere of your heart. Do not rush. Allow the Lord to lead you into the truth that He wants to show you each time you work through an exercise.

As you approach your first exercise, let me offer this word of prayer.

> Lord God, You are Creator of the Universe. You alone know the full measure of the *so much more* that you have for Your children. In the name of Jesus, I ask that You speak to the heart, mind, and spirit of these children as they sit at Your feet to seek the *so much more* of You, the *so much more* of who You created them to be, and the *so much more* of what You created them to do. Thank you in advance for Your Presence and revelation. In Jesus' name. Amen.

Exercise 1: He is Who He Says He is

Our exercises begin with the *so much more* of God. I have listed a few verses that tell a truth from Scripture, and I suggest a corresponding characteristic of God. Take the time to look up each Scripture in your Bible and ask yourself what that truth and characteristic mean for you in your life today. Write the answers in your notebook.

1. **God is all-knowing.** What does it mean to me that God knew me before He formed me?

    "Before I formed you in the womb I knew you,
    And before you were born I consecrated you" (Jeremiah 1:5).

2. **God is Creator.** Why does it matter to me that God formed me?

    For You formed my inward parts;
    You wove me in my mother's womb (Psalm 139:13).

3. **God is Intentional.** What difference does it make to me that God created me for a purpose?

    For we are His workmanship, created in Christ Jesus for good works, which God prepared beforehand so that we would walk in them (Ephesians 2:10).

4. **God is always present and active in my life.** How have I seen God work all things together for good in my life?

And we know that God causes all things to work together for good to those who love God, to those who are called according to His purpose (Romans 8:28).

5. **God is faithful.** What difference does it make that I can trust God's faithfulness to bring my call to pass?

Faithful is He who calls you, and He also will bring it to pass (1 Thessalonians 5:24).

6. Now that you have completed my short list of God's characteristics, it is time for you to list a few. Perhaps you have become particularly tuned in to God's faithfulness or His creativity. Maybe you have become more aware of His sweet kindness or His unconditional love. All of those descriptions are spot-on. We all experience God in different ways at different times. The purpose of this exercise is to open your spirit and mind to the *so much more* of God today—in the here and now. Go ahead and finish this exercise by writing down the characteristics of God that you are currently seeing in your life.

Understanding These Questions

You may be asking why a book about figuring out your identity and your purpose/destiny starts with an exercise that is all about God. The fact is there is always *so much more* for your life because, this side of eternity, there is always *so much more* of God. There is always *so much more* of His revelational truth to consume and *so much more* of His divine wisdom to glean for your life. As you seek the *so much more* of God, He will reveal *so much more* of His plan and purpose for your life.

Your Kingdom purpose is to influence, affect, and change the world right where you are. You may not immediately see how God can use you to affect change in your current situation. It can take time to first see your home, work, play, or volunteer life through God's eyes before you can get an idea of where, who, and what He is pointing out to you. That is the purpose of our next exercise.

Exercise 2: Starting Point

Every journey has a starting point. This exercise is meant to establish your starting point as we begin our journey of discovery. Take a few minutes and describe your current situation—simply create a written snapshot of your life. Are you single, married, divorced, or widowed? Do you have children, grandchildren, or great-grandchildren? Do you work outside or inside the home? Do you go to a church? Do you volunteer at a charity, school, church, or ministry? Where do you spend your free time? Who are you with the most? What do you love to do? What is your greatest strength? What are your talents? Describe your personality. You get the idea. Write the description that comes to you about your life today in your notebook.

As you move through the remaining chapters of the book, keep this snapshot that you've taken in the forefront of your mind. I would recommend that you even review it occasionally. You might find that the Lord puts His finger on one or two of the areas you've written down and says, *"This is the place and these are the people for you to shine with My Presence and to affect change on My behalf."*

CELEBRATING YOUR PROGRESS AND LOOKING AHEAD

Way to go, Dear One! You have taken the first step in your journey of discovering the *so much more* that God has for you. You were created to do great things! Your Kingdom purpose is to affect change in the world right where you live. **God longs for you to soar in the sweet spot of your identity and purpose.** As you do, you release more of Heaven into your life and into the lives of others. To ensure that nothing encumbers you on your flight of discovery, we will look next at the freedom that the Lord wants to unlock and increase for you. Your preflight inspection will clear out whatever might try to hinder your journey.

Before we take the next step, though, allow me to pray with you.

Father God, You created each of us with a special blend of characteristics to influence and change the place and people that You put in our lives. Please shine Your light on the "who," "when," and "how" of our purpose so that we can advance Your Presence in the world in which we live. In Jesus' name, we pray. Amen.

2.
Created For So Much More
FREEDOM:
Inspecting Your Instruments

Before pilots take off, they conduct a preflight inspection to ensure that everything is ready for the journey. The questions they are trying to answer include: Are all instruments working effectively? Is the radio functioning properly? Is fuel supply sufficient to reach the destination? Like pilots, our first order of business as believers preparing to soar with God, is to ensure that everything is properly aligned so that we are ready to fly into freedom.

First things first. Another adventure lies ahead. It will require your time, energy, and dedication. God is ready to speak new things to you on this part of your journey!

"Behold, the former things have come to pass, Now I declare new things;
Before they spring forth I proclaim them to you" (Isaiah 42:9).

Do you believe this promise? Are you willing to accept that the Lord has new things prepared for you AND do you have faith that before they spring forth, He will let you know about them? Are you ready to take responsibility for your future? Are you determined to set aside past understandings and recognize that the Lord may be telling you something new?

I pray that your answers to those questions were "Yes! Yes! Yes!" However, you may feel unsettled about whether you can accomplish all that the Lord requires. Let me put your heart and mind at ease. Taking a journey with the Lord is not as difficult as you might think. God meets you where you are—before you have everything figured out—and He guides you from there. He's not looking for the best of the best. When I was a senior in high school, we voted for awards called "Notables," which included titles like "Most Talented," "Most Likely to Succeed," "Most Athletic," "Most School Spirit," etc. I want to assure you that God doesn't care about those attributes. His only "Notable" is "Most Willing and Open to Receive"—the definition of a teachable spirit. With a teachable spirit, you will be able to inspect your instruments effectively and your journey ahead will be clearly marked and easily navigated. With a teachable spirit, the Lord will take you to unseen destinations. God has prepared amazing, unpredictable opportunities just for you and for each one of His children who operates with a heart to learn. The Apostle Paul describes these unique opportunities, quoting the prophet Isaiah:

> "THINGS WHICH EYE HAS NOT SEEN AND EAR HAS NOT HEARD, AND WHICH HAVE NOT ENTERED THE HEART OF MAN, ALL THAT GOD HAS PREPARED FOR THOSE WHO LOVE HIM." For to us God revealed them through the Spirit; for the Spirit searches all things, even the depths of God (1 Corinthians 2:9–10).

Your future is full of limitless possibilities when you rely on the Lord to direct your path. The spiritual journey on which we embark has life-changing possibilities. Are you ready, able, and willing to take the second step of self-inspection by pre-committing to do your part during the journey that lies ahead?

You Are Responsible for Your Future

Ezekiel 18 presents a rather interesting directive from the Lord about moving beyond the past. The words were revolutionary at the time the Lord spoke them to Ezekiel, and they still hold that same kind of power for us today—if we allow Holy Spirit to use them that way. Early in the chapter it says,

> "What do you mean by using this proverb concerning the land of Israel, saying, 'The fathers eat the sour grapes, but the children's teeth are set on edge'? As I live," declares the Lord God, "you are surely not going to use this proverb in Israel anymore" (Ezekiel 18:2–3).

Before God spoke this Word to the Israelites through Ezekiel, they had spent hundreds of years shouldering the burden of past generations' actions. With His words, "The fathers eat the sour grapes, but the **children's** teeth are set on edge" (bold emphasis mine), the Lord was saying, "No more." From that time on, He would hold each generation responsible for its own actions. The remainder of the chapter goes into great detail about the breaking of this generational punishment. Fathers would be judged on their own righteousness and unrighteousness. Sons would be judged for their own righteous and unrighteous actions.

The point that I would like you to remember is that whether or not you were dealt a bad hand, come from generations of disbelief or sin, or even have been victimized, you and you alone are responsible for your healing and living in the fullness of who you were created to be. **The choice to move forward is yours.** All too often, I see people so accustomed to the baggage of their pasts that they cannot let go of the weight of it. You are the one responsible for picking up and dragging around that overweight bag of guilt, shame, and sin that satan wants to use to burden you. You alone can choose to grab hold of what Christ did for you on the cross. With His death and Resurrection, Christ paid the price for your salvation and sanctification.

Years ago, I attended a conference where Chuck Missler, Bible scholar and teacher extraordinaire, said, "You have been saved. You are being saved. You will be saved." These words contain a powerful truth that we, as believers, need to fully grasp and keep in the forefront of our minds. You **were saved** from sin, death, and the power of satan when you said "Yes" to Jesus as your Lord and Savior—that's salvation. You **are being saved** each day as you live out your salvation daily. You **will be saved** when, at the final judgment, you are ushered into Heaven and saved from eternal damnation.

"Being saved" is a daily choice. This daily "being saved" action is what I refer to when I ask if you are ready to take responsibility for your future. It encompasses the process of doing the work of inspecting your instruments to make sure that you are free to fly into what the Lord has for you. "Being saved" is also known as sanctification. It is being transformed more and more into the image of Christ daily as we live our lives here on Earth. God gives us free will. With our free will, God gives us the ability to choose life or death.

Choose Life

Let's look at what Moses says in the Book of Deuteronomy:

> *"See, I have set before you today life and prosperity, and death and adversity; in that I command you today to love the LORD your God, to walk in His ways and to keep His commandments and His statutes and His judgments, that you may live and multiply, and that the LORD your God may bless you in the land where you are entering to possess it"* (Deuteronomy 30:15–16).

Moses was speaking to the Israelites, but his words apply to us. Notice that the word life is connected to prosperity, multiplication, and blessing. Other words that could be used to translate the word life in this passage are light and blessing. To help us remember the power of our choices, we would be wise to keep verse 19 in this chapter before us at all times.

> *"I call heaven and earth to witness against you today, that I have set before you life and death, the blessing and the curse. So choose life in order that you may live, you and your descendants"* (Deuteronomy 30:19).

We all make choices that lead to life, light, and blessing—or to death, darkness, and destruction. The word death in this verse is connected to adversity. This death is not a physical one, but instead it represents a life lived with death, darkness, and destruction. Even after our decision to choose Jesus, we have a choice to work out our salvation daily and to live transformed by the power of the cross—or, we have a choice not to do that.

You can choose to continue to go around the same mountains of sin and bondage decisions, or you can choose freedom in Christ. Even as a follower of Christ, you still need to choose to reject the lies of the enemy and embrace the truth of freedom in Christ. If you don't choose His freedom, the baggage of your past will continue to weigh you down.

Looking at what you are carrying around is foundational to your preflight inspection and can take some work on your part. Too many individuals run from ministry to ministry looking for the one quick fix that will heal all their issues. Working with ministers trained in inner healing is a wonderful path to freedom. However, it is not the ministry that heals—the Lord does. Trained ministers can help lead the way and facilitate the Lord's work. The work is ultimately between you and the Lord—and the choices you make to co-labor with what He has done, is doing, and will do—to allow the release of freedom in your life.

Keep Standing

In his letter to the Galatians, Paul challenges us to keep standing to maintain freedom once it has been received.

> *It was for freedom that Christ set us free; therefore keep standing firm and do not be subject again to a yoke of slavery* (Galatians 5:1).

We have a choice to stand in the freedom that Christ offers from the empty tomb. Or, we can make choices and decisions that open the door to allow the yoke of slavery to be placed back on us. We co-labor with Holy Spirit and Christ's freedom when we make changes in our words, lifestyles, and actions that reflect the spiritual freedom procured for us. Sometimes we need more than prayer—we need a different decision.

Each person must take responsibility for his or her own backpack. Do you find yourself burdened by a backpack of a painful past? Do you carry wounds caused by family or friends? Grief? Sin? Whatever is weighing you down in your personal backpack, let me ask you: Are you benefitting from still carrying that backpack? Do you feel affirmed when you take out the heavy rocks that you carry in that pack to discuss them with others? Living that way is not freedom! It is codependency with death, darkness, and destruction! Jesus died to set you free of those burdens.

It is so easy to lighten your load. All you have to do is repent. Give those rocks to Jesus. I encourage you to envision taking out the rocks, acknowledging their names, and handing them to your Savior. He died so that you do not have to carry those rocks! Give those rocks to Him in prayer—it works, I promise—and decide not to pick them up again!

Let me share an example of how powerful it is to surrender your burdens to Jesus. During a time of inner healing ministry, Sue gave the rocks of shame and disappointment to Jesus. He took those rocks and replaced them with joy, peace, love, and abundance. Because Sue chose to surrender her burden to the Lord, He brought the freedom that allowed her to write, "I am now free to move forward in the new things God has for me, and I am expecting open doors with opportunity to bless and be blessed."

Prayer Versus Decisions

Let me explain when you need prayer and when you need a decision. Prayer is a critical part of the believer's life and an important component of the path to freedom. Deliverance ministries and prayer do great work freeing people from satan's influence, but sometimes you need more than prayer. **Sometimes you need a decision.** Look at your habits and choices. A woman struggling with a spirit of fantasy who continues to read romance novels and watch romantic movies is making poor choices. A decision to clean out her library of reading and watching material would take her a long way on her path to freedom. A husband and father who struggles to provide for his family's financial needs, yet spends large amounts of money on hobbies like golf, hunting, or meeting the guys "for a few drinks" after work, doesn't just need prayer for financial breakthrough, he needs to make different choices. I have nothing against romance novels, romantic comedies, golf, hunting, or building relationships with friends. These recreational activities help to balance our lives. At times, however, we need to change our decisions and habits as we pray for spiritual breakthroughs. Making choices that align with our freedom in Christ enables us to receive our spiritual inheritance, which can include blessings that flow from previous generations.

Perhaps your struggle is not with your choices. Perhaps your struggle is with the legacy left to you from parents who made poor choices. All too often I hear men and women say that they want nothing to do with how their parents lived. "I don't ever want to be like my father." Or, "I pray that I am never like my mother." Statements like these can throw the spiritual baby out with the bath water.

Do not throw out your inheritance of blessings because you have come from a challenging or downright destructive past. The legacy of your parents and grandparents includes both positive and negative traits, as well as both blessings and curses. Ask the Lord to show you which aspects of your inheritance are blessings—and which are not. Even if you think you know, He may reveal hidden blessings that you hadn't thought of yet. Do not deny yourself blessings from your inheritance because of pain caused by it. Reverse any curse from previous generations by forgiving those who have gone before you, and repent of any place where you have walked in agreement with that curse. By doing so, you deny satan access, and you open your heart and spirit to the legacy, gifts, talents, and blessings that come down your family line. By building on your legacy and blessings, you are being a wise mechanic. Mechanics do not throw out valuable instruments that may just need some repair work. They fix and update these instruments so that they can continue to use them. That repairing process is choosing life, Dear One. It's not as difficult as it may seem. Holy Spirit stands by waiting to assist you with your choices. He is a powerful Helper!

As we have learned, we need to take responsibility for our choices, our actions, and our words every day. "Being saved," for the purpose of this discussion, means that wherever you are on your life journey, you must take responsibility for your future and choose life. Paul tells us how he is able to choose life in his letter to the Philippians.

I really love the way The Passion Translation puts this passage:

I admit that I haven't yet acquired the absolute fullness that I'm pursuing, but I run with passion into His abundance so that I may reach the destiny which Jesus Christ has called me to fulfill and wants me to discover. I don't depend on my own strength to accomplish this; however I do have one compelling focus: I forget all of the past as I fasten my heart to the future instead (Philippians 3:12–13, The Passion Translation, TPT).

Paul is saying that you don't have to white-knuckle any of the choices of sanctification. When he says *"I don't depend on my own strength to accomplish this"* (Philippians 3:13), he is showing his dependence upon the power of Holy Spirit to change him from the inside so that he can live a life of freedom and joy.

No matter what has happened in your past, Holy Spirit enables and empowers you to make decisions for your life that align with His purpose and plan. The very Presence of God empowers you to be who you were created to be and to do what you were created to do. It's called grace. I have adopted James Ryle's definition of grace as my own. He defines grace as the empowering Presence of God enabling you to be who you were created to be and to do what you were created to do.[1] Call on the Name and Presence of Jesus, and He will lead and direct you into all grace—each and every day.

You Are in the Right Place

After reading this far, you may be wondering how your life could become the fulfillment of your God-given destiny—the plan and purpose that God had in mind when He created you. Perhaps you look to your past decisions and think that you blew it. Let me emphatically say: **Wherever you have been, you have arrived exactly at the right place at the right time to move forward in all that God the Father, Your Creator, has for you.** Whatever you have walked through, Jesus has been right next to you every step of the way. Whoever has influenced your life up to this point, Holy Spirit can now be the One to influence you. It's like He is saying, *"It is time to take these steps to freedom and fulfillment of your destiny."* God is in the recycling business. He uses what we have been through to shape and form us. What the enemy intends for our harm, God will use for our good (Genesis 50:20).

Consider the story of Joseph found in Genesis, Chapters 37–50. His brothers threw him in a pit and sold him into slavery. I am certain that Joseph struggled with the disparity between his childhood dreams and visions and his adult life as slave and prisoner. However, there was no disparity for God. He used those years in captivity to form Joseph's character. He also used those years to teach him administrative skills. In God's timing, Joseph moved from the prison to the palace, and God transformed him from prisoner to prince. Joseph had the necessary administrative skills to live out his destiny as a leader in the land. He also developed the compassion to encounter and forgive his brothers. Never underestimate the Lord's work in your darkest seasons. He is always at work with your divine purpose in His mind.

You are the sum of all your years thus far. Do not block out or try to forget what has come before this point. Heal from your past, yes, but then consider that your past has shaped you to perfectly fit God's call on your life. You are witnessing God's redemptive hand when you hear about a woman who escaped from an abusive relationship and starts working for a domestic violence prevention organization. Another great example of redemption is the man who, let go from his job of 26 years because of a "reduction of force," turns around and offers counsel and prayer to another who has just heard the words, "We are letting you go." How about the athlete, permanently side-lined due to injury, who becomes an inspiring and motivating coach to hundreds of younger athletes? The very life circumstance that you thought had ruined you could be the springboard for your future purpose and destiny—if you make the choice to allow God to use it.

Commit

Inspect your instruments by taking responsibility. Choose life. Stand firm. For the rest of our journey together, that means commit to the process. Take the time necessary to do the exercises and to listen for the Lord's direction. Then, make the decision to follow through with whatever the Lord instructs you to do. Yes, I am asking you to set aside time now and then to be quiet, ponder, and listen for the Lord to speak. This experience may be new for some of you. It may even feel uncomfortable. But I assure you that Heavenly Father, Jesus Your Redeemer, and Holy Spirit wait to speak to you. You don't have to take my word for it, though. The following verse promises God's response:

Draw near to God and He will draw near to you (James 4:8).

As a child of God, you can trust that He longs to be in relationship with you, which means that He longs to speak to your heart, mind, and spirit. So let's connect the truths of this chapter to your life. Let's ask Holy Spirit to help with inspecting your instruments to ensure that they are properly aligned and prepared for the journey ahead.

SOARING WITH GOD

Exercise 3: Take Responsibility

Sit quietly. Clear the room and atmosphere of any distractions. As you ask yourself these questions, spend whatever time is needed to ponder and journal to answer them. Then, commit to make the necessary changes that will open the doors to your freedom, abundance, and operating more fully in your gifts and talents.

1. Am I ready to take responsibility for my future?
2. Will I commit to complete the exercises in this book?
3. Are there choices in my life that are hindering my freedom to be who God created me to be?
4. Are there decisions that I am making that keep me from stepping into the actions that God is asking me to take?

Now that you have begun to ask these questions, thank Him in advance for where He is going to take you and for how He is going to change your life.

The Past is Passed

A bit more self-inspection is necessary to prepare us to take flight. Let's look at a biblical example of how God helped a new leader learn from a previous leader's mistake to move forward.

Before the Israelites could enter the Promised Land, a death had to occur. Here is the backstory: In Numbers 20, the Lord told Moses to speak to the rock at Meribah to draw water for the Israelites. Instead of just speaking to the rock, Moses took it upon himself to do more than what God said. He took his rod and struck the rock. God then told Moses that he (Moses) would not enter the Promised Land because of his lack of faith. He was able to view the Promised Land, but he was not allowed to enter it. This punishment may seem severe, but I would say that it was right-on. Why? Because it was necessary for Moses to be called to Heaven (Deuteronomy 34:5) before Joshua (who took Moses' place as leader) could take the Israelites across the Jordan into the Promised Land.

Consider that where Moses had lacked faith in the power of the Lord,

Joshua showed faith when the other Israelite spies saw only giants. Listen in as Joshua reports back after spying out the land of Canaan.

> *"The land which we passed through to spy out is an exceedingly good land. If the LORD is pleased with us, then He will bring us into this land and give it to us---a land which flows with milk and honey. Only do not rebel against the LORD; and do not fear the people of the land, for they will be our prey. Their protection has been removed from them, and the LORD is with us; do not fear them"* (Numbers 14:7–9).

Joshua demonstrated his trust in the Lord—regardless of what his eyes saw. In spite of how the world looked, Joshua knew that the Lord would bring victory. It was necessary for leadership to pass from Moses to Joshua before the Israelites could possess the promises of God. The character traits that were needed in Moses to bring the Israelites out of Egypt and through the wilderness were not the same leadership traits that were required to move them forward in their destiny. I would go so far as to say that the personality, character, and leadership traits of Moses might have even hindered the transition and transformation of the people from wilderness-wanderers to promise-possessors.

We all have a little of Moses and a little of Joshua in us. Moses had the qualities needed to stand up to Pharaoh and lead the Israelites for 40 years in the wilderness. Joshua had all that was needed to lead the Israelites across the Jordan River, to conquer their enemies, and to possess the Israelites' new land.

The following truth is significant and important to remember: **The very qualities that brought you to this point may not be the necessary characteristics needed to take you further in your journey.** When planes were being designed to cross the sound barrier, new instruments had to be developed that could hold up under the stress of the increased speed. You, too, may need to change out your old instruments for the new equipment that the Lord has for you. Therefore, do not hold on to old habits if the Lord says let go. Also, don't add to what the Lord asks of you. Be willing to be pliable and teachable before the Lord. He will give you all that you need to move forward in your destiny, to cross your Jordan, and possess your Promised Land.

Exercise 4: Putting the Past in the Past

Your preflight inspection is coming to an end. The next step involves cleaning out the hindrances that would impair your journey to your destiny. A newly-staged play cannot be performed with last season's props and costumes. Let's get rid of what has become unnecessary for your future.

Get back to your notebook and, once again, take a few moments to sit quietly with the Lord. Let Holy Spirit gently put His finger on those aspects that need to be left this side of whatever represents the Jordan River in your life. Write down the things that He is telling you to leave behind. There is power when we write what the Lord reveals to us.

Ask yourself these questions:

1. What doubts do I need to leave on the altar before the Lord can carry me into my Promised Land?
2. When have I taken matters into my own hands and "helped the Lord," when He didn't ask for my help?
3. When the giants of my future loom in front of me, do I run in fear, or do I rely on the Lord to fight my battle?
4. What habits or traits that brought me to this point need to be surrendered to the Lord so that I may possess the promises of God?

CELEBRATING YOUR PROGRESS AND LOOKING AHEAD

Congratulations! You have come through the preflight inspection of the spiritual instruments necessary for your journey with dignity and grace. Because of your willingness to submit to the Lord's direction, you have cleared the way for Him to show you the *so much more* that He has for you. You have made a way for Him to be your air traffic controller. Like air traffic controllers in the real world, God sees what we cannot. He has the big picture in mind and always has your best interest at heart. You must be willing to seek out and listen to the One Voice that has the perspective to safely guide you onto your flight path.

Let me again turn to prayer on your behalf:

Thank You Lord, that You have met Your children in the journey of uncovering the greater freedom that You have for them to experience each and every day. Continue to show ways for them to choose life and to freely fly in all that You created them to be. In Your Son's Name, our Redeemer and Giver of Life. Amen.

3.
Created For So Much More
CLARITY:
Clearing Out Chatter

Trained public speakers know that to effectively deliver speeches, they must be in tune with the body language, facial expressions, and other nonverbal clues given by the audience. The industry calls this practice playing to your audience. It allows for flexibility of delivery for greatest impact. We all play to an audience as we observe verbal and nonverbal signals from people we respect, such as parents, teachers, or colleagues. Who that audience is and how much attention you give it determine your life choices and ultimately your destiny. Liken this audience to the air traffic controller's voice in our pilot's ears. That voice guides your decisions, whether you are aware that it does or not. **It is imperative that you take the time to clear out any chatter that interferes with hearing the voice of the One who created you and directs your flight.**

Voices of Interference
Each day you make thousands of decisions. What to eat, what to wear, where to go, and how to spend your time are just a few of the daily choices that you make. All too often, those decisions are based on others' opinions or the ongoing litany of advice, criticism, encouragement, and support that speaks to us like an air traffic controller speaks to a pilot.

I call the clamoring voices from various sources the "Greek chorus" that resides in your head. Your Greek chorus could be made up of teachers, friends, family, colleagues, or mentors. It may be made up of teachers who told you that you would never make it in their field. Perhaps it is the voice of the boyfriend or girlfriend who made fun of your talent. This Greek chorus might be made up of friends who told you not to make a move of relationship, job, house, or location because they didn't want to see you get hurt. Innumerable times, I have heard stories about people, who wanted to become professional artists, but didn't. In most of these cases, parents discouraged their artistically-inclined children from becoming professional artists because of the perceived difficulty earning a living "making art." From these examples and from your own Greek chorus, you know that because these voices are often comprised of well-intentioned people in your life, ignoring these voices is difficult. To move forward with what the Lord is calling you to be and do, however, you will need to discern what voices you are hearing, and to learn how to ignore any voices that are not from Heaven. Even though many times these internal voices are made up of others' voices, sometimes the loudest voice is your own.

Your self-talk voice often needs to be ignored as well to clearly hear the voice of the Lord. Do you recognize your self-talk voice? It's the voice that says you aren't strong enough to handle this crisis because you broke down in the middle of the last one. It can be the voice that says you can't speak in front of a large group because you are not thin enough, hip enough, or expert enough. Perhaps you hear the voice that says you don't measure up because you don't look, act, or sound like anyone else who is successful. Maybe the voice that you hear says, "Don't take risks to do what the Lord says," because so-and-so is already speaking, writing, and doing the same thing. Self-talk is as powerful as the voice of a Greek chorus. Both, if allowed, will shape how you think.

Our thoughts can motivate us or lead us into despair. Proverbs 23:7 says, *"For as he thinks within himself, so he is."* This idea, that you can cause something to happen by believing it will come true, is known as the self-fulfilling prophecy. We become what we think. Our thoughts play an important role in our daily choices. Is it any wonder that Paul warned the church at Corinth to keep watch over their thoughts and to take those thoughts captive that did not align with the truth of the Gospel?

> *We are destroying speculations and every lofty thing raised up against the knowledge of God, and we are taking every thought captive to the obedience of Christ* (2 Corinthians 10:5).

It's important to note that thoughts are to be taken captive to the obedience of Christ—not to the obedience of your ego or to the obedience of another person. We are to use self-control, a fruit/byproduct of Holy Spirit (Galatians 5:22–23) operating within us, to deny access to doubt, accusation, worry, shame, guilt, or anything that would keep us from our God-given destiny. Taking thoughts captive to the obedience of Christ transforms your self-talk or audience of one (you) to the Audience of One: Christ.

The Audience of One

As followers of Jesus and actors on this stage of life, we must learn to play to the Audience of One. What do I mean by playing to the Audience of One? Rather than listening to and playing to the Greek chorus made up of others or your own self talk, tune in to the Audience of One—note the capital letters. This One created you, redeemed you, reveals His heart to you, and guides you into all truth (John 16:13). Your Audience of One is God. He is the One who knew you when He formed you in your mother's womb (Psalm 139:13). He is the One who walks with you every step of the way (Matthew 28:20). He is the One who never leaves or forsakes you (Joshua 1:5). God is the One who placed your gifts and talents within you, and He is more interested in seeing you succeed than you are. If you want to succeed, then it makes sense to listen to the Lord to silence the voice of your Greek chorus and nullify your negative self-talk. It makes sense to clear out the chatter, to tune in to God's voice, and to play to your Audience of One.

When you play to the Audience of One, you live your life tuned to Heaven's perspective. You begin to see and hear who you are and what you are called to do from your Creator's viewpoint. Tune your ears to Heaven's frequency, and you will hear Jesus' heart for you and your life's purpose. Listen to the voice of Holy Spirit, and He will direct your path—a path that is uniquely yours.

The Audience of One may tell you to build an ark when there is no sign of rain, just like He told Noah (Genesis 6:14). He may tell you to leave your country like He told Abraham (Genesis 12:1), or He may tell you to stay right where you are and to wait for His Spirit to move, like He did with the disciples (Acts 1:4). He may tell you to march to the beat of a different drum or to march in step with other drummers. He may say *"Go!"* He may say *"Be still."* Because you have a unique purpose and destiny, the one and only audience it makes sense to listen to, follow, and play to, is your Audience of One, Your Heavenly Father; His Son, Your Redeemer; and His Spirit, the Counselor.

Sometimes what the Lord asks of us doesn't fit with conventional wisdom, like in the case of my friend Nichole. Nichole lives in Paducah, Kentucky. That part isn't unusual in itself—except that Paducah is three hours from where her hair and nail business was in Franklin, Tennessee. Every two weeks for three years, she made the drive to Franklin, my hometown at the time, for three days of work. Some said it couldn't be done, and they made a point of telling her just that. Nichole put her trust in the

Audience of One, and she successfully made a living commuting from Kentucky to Tennessee during the time the Lord had that door open for her. After she attended a conference where I presented the Audience of One, Nichole felt the Lord telling her that it was time to close her business and dedicate herself to her family in Kentucky. Knowing she was hearing her Audience of One, she silenced her own doubts and did as the Lord directed. She lives day-to-day, trusting the Lord to provide. Because of her faith and obedience, Nichole has seen miracles of God's mighty provision as well as the freedom to witness to the lost—all because she has been available to listen and follow her Audience of One.

My own story didn't require a move, but it did require a leap of faith. Early in the process of writing this book, I received responses that could have derailed me. One was, "Well, good luck with that!" Another response was, "Do you have a publisher lined up?" The third reaction was a simple lack of interest. These responses came from those close to me, and all of them could have fed the doubt that was a part of my self-talk. Responses from others, internal Greek-chorus voices, and self-talk need to be managed in light of the Lord's call. Taking my own thoughts captive and standing firmly on the Word of God—the call that came from my Audience of One—has given me power to continue to move forward. God gave me the mandate to write this book and He confirmed His word by making a way when there was no way. Now I know that God gave me the strength to relegate the voices of doubt and negative self-talk to the background where they had no influence on me. I wouldn't have been able to do that when I first heard the word from God, *"Write what I have given you."* In seed form, it was too tender to share with anyone but my most trusted allies and advisors.

I have learned how important it is to **be watchful about sharing private Heaven-sent directives**. Think of them as tender shoots of new grass. A newly-seeded lawn cannot be walked upon until the grass has time to mature. The same principle can be applied to the steps and path to which the Lord is directing you. There are times when the Lord gives you a vision or a mandate that doesn't meet the approval of friends and family around you. Guard it and take care to protect it. As Jesus said in Matthew's Gospel, *"Do not throw your pearls before swine"* (Matthew 7:6). We often stop right there and agree that, yes, we need to take care not to share ideas with people who can't appreciate them. However, the verse goes on to say, *"or they will trample them under their feet, and turn and tear you to pieces"* (Matthew 7:6). Prematurely sharing your pearl of a vision can destroy it and you. So take care, Dear One. Your vision—the pictures of you doing what you were created to do—and your destiny—God's plan and purpose for your life—are valuable treasures. Share them only with those that the Lord (your Audience of One) directs. You need to be watchful and careful here.

Holy Spirit will direct you to those who will encourage and support you, or He will give you the strength and dedication to withstand criticism and doubt. In my case, the Lord prepared me in advance for the conversations about this book. He bolstered my confidence and gave me the words to speak that would protect His call and direction. Knowing the Lord, you learn how to recognize His voice over the voices of your Greek chorus or your self-talk. Knowing Him well is part of the process of clearing out the chatter. Because hearing His voice is so important, let's look at a few more characteristics of God that make Him the best audience to which you can play.

Your Audience of One is the same God who *"causes all things to work together for good to those who love God, to those who are called according to His purpose"* (Romans 8:28). You may not see how your past or your present can be worked for your good or bring about the future you envision, but the Lord does. God is faithful and true.

God is the Protector of your vision, and He will bring your calling to fruition by directing conversations, developing relationships, and preparing your heart. God is not the one who stands in the way of your purpose and calling—but you might be. Yes, you can stand in the way of you becoming who you were created to be, and you can block yourself from doing what you were created to do. You may prevent yourself from moving forward into your purpose when you ignore your Audience of One, follow the directives of your Greek chorus, or allow negative self-talk to stop you in your tracks. To listen only to your Audience of One, you must take responsibility and clean your spiritual ears. That process is the next order of business.

SOARING WITH GOD
Exercise 5: Cleaning Your Ears
The Five "Rs"

When you feel stuck on your path, it may be time to clean out your ears. An easy way to cleanse your ears and your heart is to use what I call The Five "Rs." Keep these five "Rs" in the forefront of your mind and make it a habit to review them regularly. Let Holy Spirit guide you and you will stay clean before the Lord as you keep your ears tuned to Heaven and your Audience of

One. These five "R" words will walk you through a path of healing that opens your spirit, heart, and ears to receive all that the Lord is saying to you about who He created you to be and what He created you to do.

Take the time to ponder and pray through each of these five "Rs." If directed, write out what Holy Spirit shows you with each step.

1. **Recognize** who you need to forgive and what lies you have believed. Then forgive those you need to forgive.
2. **Repent** of believing the lies of spirits that tell you anything other than the truth that you are a treasured and gifted Child of God.
3. **Renounce** the lies of the enemy.
4. **Receive** the truth of Christ. He is the Way to Freedom, He speaks the Truth, and He brings Life (John 14:6). Everything you need is found in Him.
5. **Replace** your view of yourself and your life with God's perspective.

Exercise 6: Clearing Out the Chatter

Now, I want to take the time to clear out any voices that may interfere with hearing your Audience of One. Return to your notebook or journal and answer these questions:

1. Whose voice(s) do you repeatedly hear that direct your actions or feelings?
2. Guilt, shame, and unworthiness often come from your Greek chorus. Identify your Greek chorus by asking yourself who in your life made/makes you feel guilty, shameful, or unworthy. List the names of these people or their roles. Be as specific as you can.
3. Forgive the people whose voices you hear as part of your Greek chorus for any time that they have spoken negatively about you. Once again, it is helpful to be specific.
4. What negative self-talk do you continually speak/hear? Write out what you hear or say.
5. Take these thoughts captive to the obedience of Christ. Recognize that negative self-talk is not from Heaven. Speak the words, "I choose to take these words and thoughts captive to obedience in Christ." Taking thoughts captive often means renouncing the lies you have believed.
6. Now ask the Lord to speak the truth about the area where you were previously believing lies. Usually God's truth is the polar opposite of the

lie that you believed. For instance, say something like "God's truth says that I am His precious child and He treasures me. God's truth says that I am worthy of His blessing because I am His child. God's truth says I am a child of King Jesus; therefore, I automatically amount to something."

7. Write down the truth that He speaks to you, repeating it out loud, often. Both speaking and writing down His truth are powerful ways to replace lies with God's truth.

CELEBRATING YOUR PROGRESS AND MOVING FORWARD

Way to go! The last exercise required transparency and vulnerability before the Lord. You do not have to share anything with anyone but Him. I hope that now you feel better, lighter, and more in line with the Lord and who He created you to be. I am so proud of you! You have just cleared out the static and chatter that separates you from clearly hearing your Audience of One. Just a reminder: You can clear out the chatter of your Greek chorus and the static of your negative self-talk as often as needed through recognizing these interfering voices, repenting of believing them, renouncing lies, receiving God's truth, and replacing your vision with God's vision. You will receive clarity about your identity and purpose because you are hearing more clearly! You have shown that you are dedicated to living a life playing to the Audience of One, who created you and gave your life purpose.

Right about now you may be saying, "Okay, I get that I am supposed to be listening to God's voice for guidance and direction, but how do I know that it's God that I'm hearing and not some other influences?" Indeed, it is critical that we recognize God's voice because He is the only One we want to follow. Our next stop will have you soaring with God more intimately as you learn to more clearly recognize His voice above all others.

Before we move forward, let's pray together, sealing the work that has been done to listen to the Audience of One.

> Father, Jesus, Holy Spirit, we recognize You as the One who created us and the only One whom we should follow as we live out our purpose here on Earth. Thank You, that through Your redemptive work on the cross, we can clear out the chatter that assails us and lean in to listen and clearly hear Your voice. We honor You as our Audience of One, our Lord and Teacher. Amen.

4.

Created For So Much More
INTIMACY:
Hearing Air Traffic Control

You are awesome! You have committed to move forward in your journey to discover or rediscover your identity and destiny. You have taken responsibility and cleaned your heart, mind, and spirit from that which is hindering you from hearing the Lord. And you recognize the importance of listening solely to the voice of your Savior, your Audience of One, for guidance and direction about your purpose and destiny. In other words, your radio is tuned to Heaven's channel, and you are ready to hear more from God and experience more of the Lord. Hearing from God automatically leads you into a more intimate relationship with Him. In my years of ministry, I've found that some people tend to think that God only speaks to a select few. Others may think that He could or will speak to them personally, but that it will only happen once-in-a-while, perhaps during key moments of life. Neither scenario is true. God desires to speak to all of His children all of the time. I pray that this chapter will solidify that truth in your spirit as we consider what it takes to hear God's voice.

Faith Comes First

The first requirement to hearing God speak is faith. *"Faith is the assurance of things hoped for, the conviction of things not seen"* (Hebrews 11:1). Faith equals belief. You must believe that God will speak to you. Faith changes how, and even if, you receive what is presented to you. The writer of Hebrews shows the difference between receiving a word with faith and without faith.

> *For indeed we have had good news preached to us, just as they also; but the word they heard did not profit them, because it was not united by faith in those who heard* (Hebrews 4:2).

Two groups of Jews heard the Good News. Those who had faith received and believed the Good News and became Christ Followers. They united their faith with what they heard. Faith plays a part in hearing God's voice because when you are seeking God for direction and guidance, it is imperative that you first have the faith to believe that He will speak to you. Without faith, you will not be able to receive what is presented—and you will be like the second group of Jews in this passage that did not benefit from the saving news of Christ.

No Fear

The second requirement to hear the voice of the Lord is to live without fear of the supernatural nature of God. In the years that I have walked formally in a prophetic ministry that speaks a prayer or offers direction, confirmation, and encouragement from the Lord to others, I have been questioned and challenged by those who do not think the Lord speaks to people today. I have been called arrogant and an elitist by those who do not understand how I can say "The Lord told me…" Fear of the supernatural nature of God is one of the biggest hindrances to hearing from Him. His heart's desire is to be in intimate relationship with each of His children. How do you have a relationship without both parties speaking to each other? Living in fear of the supernatural nature of God is diminishing who God is. Paul calls it quenching the Spirit.

> *Do not quench the Spirit; do not despise prophetic utterances. But examine everything carefully; hold fast to that which is good*
> (1 Thessalonians 5:19–21).

Do not quench the Spirit. The Spirit is quenched when the fear of the supernatural won't allow the voice of God to be heard. The Amplified Bible puts it this way:

> *Do not quench (suppress or subdue) the [Holy] Spirit; Do not spurn the gifts and utterances of the prophets [do not depreciate prophetic revelations nor despise inspired instruction or exhortation or warning]. But test and prove all things [until you can recognize] what is good; [to that] hold fast*
> (1 Thessalonians 5:19–21, Amplified Bible, Classic Edition, AMPC).

In other words, do not allow fear of the unknown, of the mysterious, supernatural nature of God and His language to keep you from hearing what He is saying in this day and time. The best way to overcome that fear and recognize God's voice is to spend time with Him. Experiencing God is how you gain understanding of His language. Dedicate time to reading His Word and sitting in His Presence, and you will become better equipped to hear and know His voice (John 10:4).

Openness

Once we believe that the Lord wants to speak to us and we have let Holy Spirit rid us of any fear, our openness to receive God's message is critical. A closed fist cannot receive a gift. Likewise, a closed mind cannot receive the gift of hearing the Lord's voice in a Scripture verse, word, impression, or sign from Him. How we approach something affects what we receive from it. Jesus shows us how attitudes affect outcome in a verse in Matthew:

"He who receives a prophet in the name of a prophet shall receive a prophet's reward; and he who receives a righteous man in the name of a righteous man shall receive a righteous man's reward" (Matthew 10:41).

I have often heard this verse quoted when it comes time for the offering at prophetic events and conferences, implying that those who donate to the prophetic ministry will be blessed financially. I believe a prophet's reward is not a financial blessing, but that the reward comes in hearing from the Lord. I think a better understanding of this verse lies in describing prophetic art and language.

Paintings speak different ideas to different people. If a person looks at a painting as a "pretty picture," that is the level of enjoyment that will be received (a righteous man's reward). If, however, someone who is open to Holy Spirit asks, "What do You want to say to me through that painting?", a deeper message and meaning—or a prophet's reward—will be received.

I demonstrate that people can in fact receive a deeper message from art at my conferences. I have audience members ask the Lord to speak to them through my paintings, which I bring with me to display in the room. The revelations people receive have been fascinating to say the least, but I'll share just one example here. Most of my paintings are abstract in nature. Lynn, an attendee at one of my conferences, told me that she had never understood abstract paintings. She also reported that she began her conversation with the Lord by saying, "I don't see anything but a mess of colors." Despite her initial skepticism, she still was open as she sought Him. The Lord responded and showed her faces within the painting and then spoke to her spirit saying, *"This is a picture of what you do. When others see messes, you see faces and minister to them."* These words were an amazing affirmation to her because she runs a ministry that works with those re-entering society from prison.

Just like being open to hearing from the Lord through a painting, we can receive the same type of prophetic reward if we are open to hearing God's language. If we sensitize our spirits, minds, and hearts to receive from Heaven, many common and often overlooked signs, images, and messages will become more than "pretty pictures." Deeper meanings and applications become obvious when we simply open ourselves to ask the Lord, "What do You want to say to me through this?" Let me give you another example from my life when I heard a deeper meaning from the Lord. Years ago, it seemed that whenever I looked at the clock, it read 11:11. Because the number 11 is often considered to be a number of incompleteness, it bothered me a little, so I would periodically ask the Lord about it. Then, one day in the car—God loves to speak to me while I'm driving—I heard Him say, *"It's because I'm not done with you yet."* To this day, whenever I see the time 11:11, I smile and am reminded that my life is always in a state of becoming who I was created to be.

Accessorize, Follow, or Engage

As a professional artist, I find that most art buyers make art purchases for one of three reasons: to accessorize, to follow, or to engage. The first group is made up of those who buy to "match their sofas." They are more interested in home accessories than in the quality of or the story behind the art. The second group includes those who purchase what friends, designers, or magazines tell them to buy—in other words, this group follows trends and people. The third group is comprised of those who allow themselves to engage with the art and the artist. They are interested in the title, the story, and the interpretation of the painting. Their hearts are open to receive what the painting offers in terms of inspiration and message. The story of Lynn seeking the Lord and seeing faces in the midst of an abstract painting is a great example of being open to engage with art. Another example of being engaged with art occurred when a couple bought a beach scene painting of mine because the painting reminded the woman of a trip that she had taken to Ireland with her mother. As she pointed just beyond the edge of the canvas, she said, "Mom's sitting right there."

The same options of accessorizing, following, and engaging are available in your relationship with the Lord. In day-to-day life, you can set aside your relationship with God so that it stays in a box, on the table, on a book shelf, or in the four walls of the church on Sunday mornings. In other words, God can become an ACCESSORY to your life.

Secondly, like those who followed trends and others' opinions with their art purchases, you could choose to FOLLOW what your friends, family, or church doctrine tell you about God without thinking much about Him. When you do that, you are simply following what others say and teach, but you aren't initiating your own interaction with Him.

A third option is to choose a relationship—to ENGAGE with Jesus, your Shepherd—so that you are open to receive His word and revelation when He speaks. Openness to receive engages Holy Spirit and invites Him to speak. He is a gentleman. For the most part, He will only enter your life as far and as intimately as you allow. He is a respecter of boundaries and will not usually cross the lines that people put in place. Those boundaries can be as basic as unbelief that He speaks today or as subtle as placing expectations on how He should speak to you.

Hindrances to Hearing

You can have faith, be open to receive, be engaged with the Lord, and still get in the way of hearing His voice when you expect that He will speak to you in the same manner that He speaks to one of your sisters or brothers in Christ. Not only does this comparison open the door to envy, jealousy, and a host of destructive thoughts, feelings, and spirits, but also you miss what the Lord is saying because you have tried to put what He says and how He communicates in a box. If there is one thing I know about God, it's that you can't put anything that has to do with Him in a box!

During personal ministry, I often see breakthroughs once individuals let go of their preconceived notions and stop trying to put God's ways or words in a box. Here's just one example. William had strayed from an intimate relationship with the Lord. Any time he would try to think his way closer to Jesus, he would end up seeing a white brick church building, traditional in style. It left him uninterested in seeking God because the message seemed to be that God could only be found within the four walls of a traditional church.

Ultimately, William came to me seeking prayer ministry for freedom in a particular area of his life. It was obvious that before Christ could bring freedom, this young man needed to recommit to the Lord and to see himself as the Father saw him. During our time of ministry, the vision of the church building changed to a night sky full of stars where William met Heavenly Father on the moon. As William began to open his heart to receive more of the Lord, the picture morphed to one of the universe.

God showed William, in a very personal way, that although He indeed can be found within the four walls of a church, Father, Son, and Holy Spirit were as big as the universe, and they could not be contained within the four walls of any church building. What a great visual of God's messages breaking down a preconceived box about God with unique language specifically tailored to the needs of His child! The universe is His and He will use every bit of it to reach His children. Since God doesn't have just one way to speak, we must use discernment to recognize His voice.

Discerning the Voice of the Lord

Whenever I teach about hearing the voice of God, I am almost always asked, "How do I know it is God speaking and not me?" Allow me to share one of my personal experiences to help provide an answer.

A couple years ago, I took a day trip to ride along as others fished in the Gulf of Mexico. One of the lessons that I learned out on the Gulf was that fishermen search for signs. They look for birds, porpoises, jumping fish, and/or a churning of the water to indicate that fish are in a certain area. They know those signs because they know the ways of the sea. Their eyes are trained to see shifts in the currents, the depth of the water, and much more. Knowledge and understanding come from studying charts, staying tuned-in to weather patterns, training with those who have more experience, and experiencing the cycles of nature for many years.

The same principles can be applied to reading the signs of Heaven as well as discerning and understanding God's language. Knowledge and understanding come from studying His Word, staying tuned to the times and the seasons, and learning from those further down His path than we are. God's language is not one that is easily taught. It takes time to experience the many facets of God and His ways of speaking.

The following truth to remember is the single most helpful piece of advice I can offer about hearing the voice of the Lord: **God is not human; He is Spirit.** That means His first language is not English. It isn't even Hebrew or Greek. It is spirit language. Spirit language uses whatever it takes to communicate.

God's Spirit may speak through pictures and feelings. He might bring a perception or a sense of His Presence. His language is heart language, which sometimes means a knowing, or a "niggling." He speaks in parables and analogies, metaphors and similes. His proficiency of language is limitless—we can't predict how He speaks to us. We must open both our hearts and minds to receive what He is saying in unusual and even supernatural ways.

If God speaks in spirit language, then having at least a working knowledge of interpreting His language is important for translating Heaven's language into Earth's language. Let's dig into what is known in charismatic circles as "the prophetic." In the broadest sense of the word, this term means divinely-inspired messages. Notice the word "messages." God's ways are not our ways (Isaiah 55:8), and He uses innumerable methods to communicate with His children. However, when He chooses to speak, our loving God speaks in languages that can be heard and understood by His children.

Your Creator knows you better than you know yourself, and He knows exactly how to speak to you to ensure that you hear His message. The language He chooses to speak to you will be a different language than what He uses to speak to me. God spoke to my young friend William through pictures. I am more of an "intuit-er," meaning that I get a sense or a knowing about things. In other words, before I understand exactly what God is trying to say, I catch on that He is speaking. Anticipating that He wants to speak sensitizes my antennae and opens my spirit to receive and interpret what Holy Spirit is saying. God speaks to my husband through the process of due diligence. In the midst of doing work, Rick will get a feeling of peace and a sense that God is saying, *"This is the way, walk in it"* (Isaiah 30:21). These examples help prove the point: **You are uniquely made and the Lord has His unique way of speaking to you.**

Interpreting God's Language

Hearing God's message can take any number of forms and may require interpretation, especially if the message is to be shared. When I am ministering prophetically, I will often see an image or a scene. There are times when a word will come to my spirit that is not in my usual vocabulary. Other times, I will be overwhelmed with emotion. All of these instances require that I seek the Lord to show me the meaning of what I am seeing, hearing, or feeling before I share verbally what I am receiving from Holy Spirit. All of these are examples of spirit language being interpreted into English in order to be spoken.

Think of interpreting God's language like interpreting a parable. In Matthew 13, the disciples asked Jesus why He spoke in parables. His response was:

"Because it has been given to you to know the mysteries of the kingdom of heaven, but to them it has not been given. For whoever has, to him more will be given, and he will have abundance; but whoever does not have, even what he has will be taken away from him. Therefore I speak to them in parables, because seeing they do not see, and hearing they do not hear, nor do they understand" (Matthew 13:11–13).

Parables can be described as stories or illustrations using everyday objects, situations, and relationships to point to a greater, deeper truth. They should compel listeners to hunger for more, to discover truth, and apply it to their lives. In the same way that parables cause a thirst for more of God's truth, a message from Heaven should always lead us back to Heaven.

Holy Spirit uses everyday objects, situations, and relationships to guide and direct us to God's Kingdom purposes here on Earth. The world is His dictionary and He uses it all. You may be familiar with such commonly understood prophetic language like rainbows signifying God's promises and butterflies symbolizing the arrival of something new in life, like a new job, a child, or a spouse. God often uses nature to speak to His children. Sunsets, cloud formations, and even rainfall often speak to the hearts of those open to receive. Sunsets can speak of God's creativity and His vast Presence. For many, rain symbolizes the Presence of the Holy Spirit. Many have seen angelic shapes and wings in cloud formations, offering peace in the midst of a stormy season of life. These cloud formations are often interpreted as helpful signs letting people know that God's angelic army is ministering to them in the midst of the crisis. For me personally, the presence of hawks or eagles equates with the Presence of God, reminding me that I never travel this life alone.

God brings revelation to our lives and our purpose through numerous ways that we can't predict. I will say it again: The world is God's dictionary and He will use whatever He needs to get His message across! Some of His words or promptings are clear; some are more mysterious and in need of clear interpretation. Sometimes, God's messages can be as obvious as a traffic light where red means stop and green means go. Other times, God's messages can seem initially vague, and they require asking Him for clarification over time.

For several years, my husband and I were looking for a different home. We had traveled down many paths. Two years ago, we were led to purchase land and build our home. Everything was a "green light" until it wasn't. Ultimately, at the end of a lengthy process, we were given an ultimatum and were told that in order to build a home in the neighborhood, we would have to build a style of home that did not suit us. That undesirable situation was as clear as a red traffic light. That neighborhood was not the one for us. Our first reaction was to want to fight for our rights. Instead, however, as difficult as it was, we put our faith in the Lord and walked away from that dream. Today, I can honestly say that we are grateful for His wisdom and guidance even though we didn't understand it at the time. In that house-hunting incident, God spoke clearly to us. I have, however, had different experiences with His messages not being so clearly packaged.

God's messages often come wrapped in the mysterious. Like a hidden treasure, His message can require a treasure map and a willingness to search for the meaning. Holy Spirit took me on this type of treasure hunt just last week. The condo where I am staying as I write is in a neighborhood surrounding a marina. My daily walk often takes me through the area where boats are dry-docked. Hundreds of boats are lined up, one after the other. The other day as I walked through the marina, the boat that was front and center as I exited the area was named "Contender." My spirit leapt a bit, but I walked on. The next time I walked through the marina, the boat was in the same place. Once again, my spirit leapt, and I knew that the Lord was speaking. All I could hear was my husband's imitation of Marlon Brando in the movie, *On the Waterfront,* saying, "I could have been a contender." The words I heard meant nothing to me in the moment. It took digging in, researching the various meanings of the word, along with much thought and prayer, before I understood what Papa—how I often refer to God the Father—was trying to tell me.

When I looked up the word contender, I found this definition "one that contends; especially: a competitor for a championship or high honor."[2] It took prayer and pondering with the Lord before I realized what He was showing me: I had the skills and expertise to write this book. God's meaning wasn't initially obvious, but with greater searching for that meaning, I felt His pleasure, His love, and even more encouragement for His current assignment for me.

This story from my own life shows the importance of being open to receive something from the Lord at any time. I could have easily walked on by and not experienced the blessing of God's smile and additional vote of confidence. As it was, my antennae were sensitive to the whispers and directives from Heaven. I committed to searching out what the Lord wanted to say, and was blessed immeasurably through the process. One of those blessings was drawing closer to God to understand His whisper.

It is a beautiful experience to explore the mysterious language of God for its message and meaning. Albert Einstein said, "The most beautiful thing we can experience is the mysterious. It is the source of all true art and science."[3] I was inspired by that quote and wanted to expand it to apply to hearing God's voice. The Deborah Gall version is: "God's language is mysterious—it is supernatural and it is a beautiful thing." Time spent pondering, searching, and praying about His Word and messages brings us into His Presence and into a closer relationship with Him. God uses prophetic language to purposefully conceal matters for a time so that we come to Him.

It is the glory of God to conceal a matter,
But the glory of kings is to search out a matter (Proverbs 25:2).

The word "glory" here is translated from the Hebrew word "kâbôd." It is the same word used for God's Presence in the cloud by day and the fire by night, which went before the Israelites through the wilderness (Exodus 13:21). It is the same glory that filled the tabernacle (Exodus 40:34), which was the structure that served as a site of worship and the dwelling of God, while the Israelites wandered in the wilderness. When God conceals a matter and when we as His kings search out a matter, we enter into His Presence. That is right where He wants us.

Relationship over Message

Father, Son, and Holy Spirit are far more concerned about the intimacy of our relationship with Them than They are concerned about the message itself. Herein lies a most important fact about knowing when God is speaking: You must be in relationship with Him. **You have to know the One who speaks to recognize His voice and the *so much more* that He has for you.**

God will always line up His Word, His will, and His ways. The Bible— His Word—is your source for deepening your understanding of God. Scripture is your best filter for listening, interpreting, and confirming what you hear. Not every little thing will be found exactly as you would like it to be in Scripture. Therefore, knowing Father, Jesus, and Holy Spirit well is important to help you discern whether a "word" sounds like Them. If you really know a person, you know when something sounds like Them or not.

As you describe others you know, you have likely said, "That sounds just like that person." Or perhaps you were defending a friend from a false accusation, and you said, "That doesn't sound like my friend at all." In the Gospel of John, Jesus says:

> *I have called you friends, for all things that I have heard from My Father I have made known to you* (John 15:15).

The implied promise in this verse is that if you are a friend of God—meaning a believer who is dedicated to following the Lord—you already know Him well enough to recognize His voice because He has made His voice known to you. One of the best paths to more easily recognizing God's voice is to get to know Him even better. No matter how long you have walked with the Lord, there is always *so much more* to learn about who He is and how He sounds.

Knowing the Lord is the crucial key to understanding and interpreting His language. You must know Him to recognize His truth. Asking the question, "Does this sound like God?" is a great first step in interpreting a message that you feel is from Heaven. Your relationship with Him is different than anyone else's, and the language you share grows from that unique relationship.

Like identical twins who often have their own "twin speak" language, you and the Lord have your own style of communication, developed over your days, weeks, and years of growing in intimacy. God's language changes from person to person, from age to age, and from situation to situation. His vocabulary is vast, and He speaks in as many different dialects as there are people on the planet. You carry a unique pair of lenses with which to look at life. In fact, you even hear on a one-of-a-kind, unique frequency that is only heard by the two of you. Becoming aware of your special God connection/language will help you recognize when God is speaking.

Living with the knowledge and understanding that God is always speaking helps you get through the grind of every day, but knowing that He is speaking in the midst of tragedy is paramount. Several years ago, a young couple faced critical emergency surgery after a water skiing accident fractured the husband's neck. When the hospital posted the time of his surgery, the clock read 3:33. That didn't mean anything to those of us waiting with the wife, but those three digits meant the world to her. It was a time stamp that was a special kiss from Heaven for her and her husband. They had invited the Lord to walk and talk with them in their daily life and continually saw the time 3:33 at significant moments.

In that anxious moment at the hospital, Jehovah Rapha, the Lord who Heals, revealed Himself to this faithful wife, showing her that He was in control and all would be well. God spoke in a language that was familiar and intimate to her. She recognized it because she knew and walked with the Lord regularly. I am happy to report that she interpreted God's language correctly. All was indeed well. What could have been a life-threatening or, at the very least, a life-changing tragedy, ended up being an incredible testimony of the Lord's hand of protection and healing power. Through the whole process, God continued to speak to the couple in their unique language, bringing encouragement and hope. God is always speaking encouragement and hope—even when we can't hear His voice.

When God Seems Silent

I can't tell you how many times I have heard people complain that God is no longer speaking to them, yet I clearly hear His voice in the story they tell. Only when I point out how He has spoken in their telling of their stories do they understand that He hasn't stopped speaking. Instead, He has just switched dialects. This "switch" happened to the Prophet Elijah. Previously, God had revealed Himself to Elijah in the wind, through earthquakes, and in fire. This day was different. God switched languages when He revealed Himself in the sound of a gentle blowing, in stillness, in a still, small voice.

So He said, "Go forth and stand on the mountain before the LORD." And behold, the LORD was passing by! And a great and strong wind was rending the mountains and breaking in pieces the rocks before the LORD; but the LORD was not in the wind. And after the wind an earthquake; but the LORD was not in the earthquake. After the earthquake a fire, but the LORD was not in the fire, and after the fire a sound of a gentle blowing (1 Kings 19:11–12).

If God seems silent to you, perhaps He is trying to teach you a different language. Do not be discouraged. Even though the Lord spoke to Elijah differently than in the past, Elijah recognized the One who was speaking. Do not look to how others hear the Lord. *"Draw near to Him and He will draw near to you"* (James 4:8). Quiet your anxiety and rest in His Presence. Trust that He wants to speak to you as much as you want to hear from Him. God has multiple ways to communicate with you and He is persistent.

> *"Indeed God speaks once,*
> Or *twice,* yet *no one notices it.*
> *"In a dream, a vision of the night,*
> *When sound sleep falls on men,*
> *While they slumber in their beds,*
> *Then He opens the ears of men,*
> *And seals their instruction"* (Job 33:14–16).

Ask the Lord to open your ears and seal your instruction. He will make sure you get the message. To better understand your unique language, perspective, and interpretation, complete the next exercise. It serves as a great springboard to help you recognize how the Lord uniquely communicates with you.

SOARING WITH GOD

Exercise 7: Tuning In

Several years ago, I was reading from the classic devotional book, *My Utmost for His Highest* by Oswald Chambers.[4] The truth I read one day struck me so deeply that I paraphrased it and painted the following words on a board: "Take a truth, give it expression, speak it clearly and boldly." I keep this board on my desk to inspire me as I work. This exercise replicates each step in that truth that I painted. You will be giving expression to a list of emotions, ideas, and truths. Be bold.

You can do this exercise in various ways. You could grab some crayons and draw. Perhaps you'd rather stand up, shake yourself out, and dance expressively. Or you could simply grab a piece of paper and write what thoughts, phrases, or word pictures come to mind. Tap into your inner-child—remember your childlike faith—and have some fun!

To start, just briefly think about how you would interpret the following list of words. Perhaps instead of drawing with the crayons, you just grab a crayon to represent the color of each word. The sky is the limit here—there is no right or wrong interpretation. There is only "your" spirit language.

Move quickly through the list and act on the first thing that comes to your mind. Write, draw, dance, select a color, sing, or speak—but write a record of what comes to you first for you to refer to later. This exercise works in the same way that an orchestra tunes to a single note. It is meant to sensitize and tune your heart and mind to the language of the spirit. By checking in with your own heart and spirit, you automatically become more in tune with Holy Spirit when He speaks.

For example: What color represents anticipation to you? If you were to dance to express joy what would the movement look like? If you were simply to draw a type of a line to express comfort, what would it look like—curvy, straight, spiral? Ready to try it? Go!

- Anticipation
- Joy
- Comfort
- Anger
- Hope
- Faithfulness
- Control
- Surrender
- God the Father
- Jesus
- Holy Spirit

Just like each of our responses to this exercise will be different, our experiences of hearing God's voice can be vastly different. Perhaps you are beginning to see that your language is more dance than words, or pictures rather than paragraphs. The key is to become aware that God is speaking to you all the time. Like radio waves that fill the air but are only heard if our instruments are turned on and tuned in, God is always speaking. It is our responsibility to align our hearts and spirits with Him to receive His messages.

God is always communicating to His children. It is our job to sensitize our antennae to receive what the Spirit is saying. One way we do that is to recall times and situations when we have heard the Lord. Revelation 19:10 says, *"For the testimony of Jesus is the spirit of prophecy."* This verse tells us that when we give Jesus credit for what He has done in our lives, we are prophesying that He will do it again. Recognizing the times that you have heard the Lord is the point of the next exercise.

Exercise 8: Recognizing His Voice

I want you to take time here and now to recognize the times, places, and results when you "heard" the Lord. In so doing, you invite Him to speak to you in the future. So, get out your notebook or journal, and let's get started.

1. Form three columns on your page.
2. Ask Holy Spirit to direct your thoughts and memories to reveal times when you heard from Him. These thoughts or memories could be as subtle as a faint impression or as bold as a large billboard. **Write whatever comes to mind in the far left column.** List as many as you can. If you have been walking with the Lord and hearing from Him for a long time, allow Him to highlight the times that He wants you to focus on at this time, and write those memories.
3. With each instance, recall the place and the situation, and **write a brief description encompassing those basics in the middle column.** You might make a note of how you were feeling at the time. Were you in prayer? Alone? Listening to music? Keep the third column blank for now.

Hold on to this page. We'll return to it with our next exercise. Meanwhile, good for you! You have testified about various times that Jesus has spoken to you and you have opened the doors and windows of Heaven to hear His voice again. You may have also begun to see a pattern of how God speaks to you, and when He speaks again in that way, you will more easily recognize it. It is important to stay aware of when, how, and what the Lord speaks, because it is an ongoing process in your life. When God speaks to you, it's like a message is pulled from Heaven and applied to your daily life.

Faith in Action

Recognizing, listening, and remembering when you have heard the voice of the Lord is how you hold on to that which is good.

Do not quench the Spirit; do not despise prophetic utterances. But examine everything carefully; hold fast to that which is good (1 Thessalonians 5:19–21).

Continue to ponder and pray over what you hear so that you can act upon it in your life. That ongoing experience is soaring with God, which enables you to know more intimacy with God and to discover the *so much more* that He has for you. Listening and interpreting are the first two steps of prophecy, or hearing God's messages for your life. Applying what those messages say and mean to your life is the final step in the prophetic process. Without application, the message cannot open up the *so much more* that God has for you.

Think of the times when you have tried to read a book when you were tired or distracted. You found yourself rereading the same paragraph over and over because it didn't "sink in." That's how it is with revelation that does not lead to application in your life. Revelation and interpretation without life application nullifies the message. It may be a good "word." It may even reveal more of who Father, Jesus, and Holy Spirit are, but if it is not put into some kind of action in our lives, it is almost worthless. Does this claim about a word from God becoming worthless sound a little heretical? After all, I have said before that God is highly concerned about intimate relationships. I would challenge you here to understand that a closer relationship with God is meant to affect your heart, which in turn changes your life. I would suggest that a greater understanding of Father, Son, or Holy Spirit's words should at least be shared with a trusted few to encourage others and to sharpen your spiritual senses. However, be aware that God's words may also be given to enable large paradigm shifts in your life.

Revelation or a prophetic word, sign, or message should always lead you closer to the Lord in a way that affects your daily life. It should be like salt that causes you to thirst for more, to ask, "What does this mean for my life today?" Apply what the Lord teaches you to your daily life and you will begin to change the world right where you live. Go where He directs you and you will experience the *so much more* that He has for you. Move forward in your journey as He directs your steps and you will soar with God in surprising and adventurous ways.

It is time to give God recognition for those times when you have heard His word and acted upon it. By doing so, you are once again taking time to testify to what Jesus has done in your life and thereby prophesying that He will continue to act on your behalf. You are also giving witness to your actions and are therefore proclaiming your desire to continue to co-labor with Holy Spirit.

Exercise 9: Application

On your page with three columns from the last exercise, consider the application of the times you heard the Lord. What changed? What resulted from the message from Holy Spirit? How did you experience the *so much more* of God and/or the *so much more* for which you were created? Ask the Lord to reveal the results, whether tangible, emotional, or spiritual. **Write what He says down in the blank third column.**

As you reflect on these moments offer a prayer of thanksgiving and give Jesus the glory. In doing so, you are once again prophesying into your future.

CELEBRATING YOUR PROGRESS AND MOVING FORWARD

Congratulations, my friend! Now you understand that to hear and understand the Lord's voice, you must recognize and experience ways that He speaks and operates. You are beginning to experience that before you can move into the *so much more* for your life you must become more familiar with the *so much more* of God. You know that He is not a puppet master who manipulates us. You are seeing the truth that He is not a faceless, exalted, and disconnected divine-being who sits idly by watching the world He created. You are learning that He is a God of intimate relationship. He is faithful and loving, and He wants to walk with you daily. He longs to be found by you.

You will seek Me and find Me when you search for Me with all your heart (Jeremiah 29:13).

I love this passage in Jeremiah. It reminds me of a loving father playing hide-and-seek with his child, waiting expectantly to be found so that he can hug and delight in his child. That's the way God the Father longs to be found. He waits expectantly to love on and delight in you. I know He has *so much more* for you, Dear One. I also know He can't wait to show it to you as you sit at His feet, and tune your ears, your heart, and your spirit to Heaven. He longs for you to soar in intimacy with Him, so draw near to God. Your Father, Savior, and Comforter will speak of the *so much more* that awaits. Wait as They confirm your direction and soar with them as they give you more certainty for your future.

First, before we move on, let's take time to thank the Lord and worship Him in prayer.

Thank You Lord, that You promise to draw near to us and to speak to Your children. We worship You as an intimate and loving Creator, Redeemer, and Spirit, Who longs to walk beside us and guide us into the destiny that You have purposed for our lives. We embrace Your supernatural ways and look forward to learning more of who You are as we move forward in this journey. In Your Son's name, we pray. Amen.

5.
Created For So Much More
CERTAINTY:
Confirming Your Flight

As Holy Spirit whispers His love, thoughts, and plans for your future, you begin to see what makes up your very own *so much more*. To ensure that you won't run with partial vision, it is important to spend time to confirm God's direction and vision for your life. As you read God's signs, listen to His language, and interpret His messages, be sure to hold things loosely until He confirms His word.

The German fairy tale of *Hansel and Gretel* told by The Brothers Grimm gives a good picture of using successive confirmations to help you find your way. The children left bread crumbs as they walked through the forest to find their way home. My husband and I have often used that fairy tale as the basis of our prayer "Lord, give us bread crumbs to show us our path." When you don't have a clear picture of direction, asking the Lord for the next step—or the next bread crumb—is a great prayer. Let me offer a word of caution here: There is truth in the adage, "All that glitters is not gold." Make no mistake about it, satan can throw bread crumbs along your path to distract and mislead you. Keeping your ears tuned to the voice of Heaven will drown out the distraction of other voices and will give you discerning eyes. You will recognize the difference between God's bread crumbs and satan's fool's gold. Asking the Lord for confirmation is one way to gain discernment and stay on the trail that the Lord has blazed for you.

Confirming appointments, dates, flights, hotel reservations, routes, and traffic conditions is a wise step for any journey to ensure that you get where you are going and have someplace to stay once you get there. It is even more important to confirm messages sent from Heaven to understand and grab hold of what the Lord has for you. Trust me, taking the time to receive confirmation is not delaying your destiny. I would never want to hold you back from your destiny! I am, however, actually helping you ensure that the steps you are taking are God's steps. Proverbs 16:9 says, *"The mind of man plans his way, But the LORD directs his steps."* God knows the whole picture. He sees the puzzle put together. Let Him direct your steps and confirm the pieces that He wants to share with you.

Paul writes, *"For we know in part and we prophesy in part"* (1 Corinthians 13:9). On this side of eternity, we only see/hear/sense in part. Revelation from Heaven may bring a glimpse, a nugget, or a piece of the puzzle to us, but only the Lord has the whole picture. I honestly believe He hands out pieces/parts to keep us relying on Him for more. No matter the size of the revelation, we must know if what we are hearing, seeing, and sensing is indeed coming from the Throne Room. We must also discern if the word is meant as a directive for action.

I offer only a few ways to confirm God's revelation. Whether spoken to you by someone else or spoken directly from Heaven to your spirit, getting confirmation is a necessary step and requires time in His Presence. Our Lord's methods for confirming His directions, plans, and purposes are as vast as the dialects He speaks. The following methods are meant to help you gain more confidence, but are in no way meant to limit God's ways of bringing confirmation.

Read the Signs

God is always talking. It is your responsibility to tune your antenna to clearly hear His voice. The Lord will use anything in your life to speak to you and confirm His words to you. Ask Him for wisdom and discernment to not only see the signs, but also to be able to comprehend them. Watch for sign posts along the road, and—like bread crumbs—they will line your path.

Most of you know how to "read" a traffic light. Red lights/red flags mean stop. Green light means go. Yellow lights mean caution. For our purposes here, I want to underline the point that the green light means go as long as it stays green. You don't stop at a green traffic light because it might turn red. You continue through the intersection. The same principle about not stopping is true in your spiritual life. We are to interpret God's signs in the same way; a green light means go until it turns yellow or red. It can be difficult to understand when the Lord turns a green light to red, but it is not our understanding that concerns God. Obedience is the key when the Lord tells you to go—or to stop/wait/hold. Trust that He is sovereign in your life, remember that His ways are not your ways, and know that His thoughts are higher than your thoughts (Isaiah 55:9). His perspective is much broader than yours. During these times when His signals seem to change unexpectedly, we often scratch our heads and say, "Really, Lord?" Nevertheless, walk on in obedience.

I have shared before that my husband and I were on an arduous journey to find a different home. A number of times, we got quite a distance down a path to a particular purchase when the green light suddenly turned red. One such time came down to my husband making one more phone call. I was gone at the time, but when I came home and he told me what he had discovered we knew—once again—the Lord was saying *"Not this one."* As disappointing as that was, we both felt peace about walking away from that purchase, which confirmed that we were to say "Yes" to God's sign and "No" to that particular house. Having peace is one of the strongest confirmations of the Lord.

Where's Your Peace?

Peace is a powerful sign from Holy Spirit. One of my most often used pieces of advice to those I coach is "Don't move unless you have peace." This principle applies to a move of any kind. Don't take a job or a gig. Don't marry or even go on a date if you don't have peace about the person. Don't say yes to an interview, lunch date, or volunteer opportunity if you have uncertainty in your spirit or questions in your heart. That is not peace. Wait for the peace that passes human understanding, as Paul wrote to the Philippians. It is what will *"guard your hearts and minds in Christ Jesus"* (Philippians 4:7).

Peace is a sure sign that you are on the right path. Many other checkpoints also determine whether a word or direction is from the Lord and is meant to be acted upon. Here are a few more checkpoints to help guide you.

Personal Witness

Closely related to finding your peace is personal witness. You may have heard the phrase "That bears witness in my spirit." What does that mean? Let me shed some light on the topic. Holy Spirit abides in you. His Spirit is at work within you. The moment when something bears witness in your spirit may feel like an aha moment. You may think, "Why haven't I thought of that before?" Or, it could be that you are filled with awe and excitement about what the Lord has in store. I doubt that Mary felt "peace," as we understand it, when the angel Gabriel gave her the news that she would give birth to Jesus. Her spirit, however, must have given witness/confirmation to the word of God, or she wouldn't have been able to say, *"Behold, the bondslave of the Lord; may it be done to me according to your word"* (Luke 1:38).

The opposite emotions of peace apply for NOT bearing witness—you may feel confusion, tension, and stress. Handle uncertainty carefully, however. Prophecy is often calling forth those things that are not as if they are. God may surprise you. Hold things that are not in your comfort zone loosely and allow the Lord to filter and confirm the word. To use our house-buying analogy, eventually we felt the Lord telling us to lay all of our "must haves" at His feet and to shift our paradigm. When we opened ourselves to going out of our comfort zone, He showed us the home where we now live. The new home required us to move to another area of Nashville. Although we had questions and didn't really understand why, God confirmed this direction with a personal witness as He unified us in our knowledge and commitment to a new area. **If there are any negative impressions regarding a word, don't act on it.** Let it sit. The Lord is faithful to you and to His word, and He will make sure you get His message.

Test the Spirit

Testing the spirit behind a word or revelation is an important step to confirm that the word is from God. The Apostle John put it this way:

> *Beloved, do not believe every spirit, but test the spirits to see whether they are from God, because many false prophets have gone out into the world. By this you know the Spirit of God; every spirit that confesses that Jesus Christ has come in the flesh is from God; and every spirit that does not confess Jesus is not from God* (1 John 4:1–3).

The first question to ask to test the Spirit is where does the "word" point? Another way to ask this question is, "Who is elevated or made to look important?" In Luke 1:37, when Gabriel prophesies to Mary, *"For nothing will be impossible with God,"* he points to the Lord. Gabriel is neither taking credit for the prophecy nor is he elevating Mary. He is giving God the credit for the miracle of which he prophesies. In other words, the prophetic word should cause the listener or reader to turn to the Lord in thanksgiving and for guidance. Gabriel's deflection of the attention back to the Lord made it possible for Mary's spirit to witness to the word of Gabriel even though it must have felt impossible to her. It doesn't matter if the word you hear is in your quiet time or if someone else speaks a word to you. If it points to the

Lord, it is likely from Him. Similarly, anything that sets itself (or you) above the Lord is not from Him.

Purpose

Another way to confirm if a prophetic word is right and true is to consider its purpose. In other words, ask yourself what is the purpose/intent of the revelation? One of the "go-to" Scriptures for understanding prophecy is 1 Corinthians 14. In this chapter, Paul tells us that the purpose of prophecy, meaning divinely-inspired messages, is for encouragement, edification, or comfort.

But one who prophesies speaks to men for edification and exhortation and consolation (1 Corinthians 14:3).

God loves you, honors you, and respects you. Anything that would hurt, harm, or hinder you emotionally, spiritually, or physically is not from the Lord. You can see from the last two methods that Scripture is incredibly valuable as a filtering tool.

Scripture Witness

I am amazed at how practical the Scriptures can be. God has used His Word to confirm things for me that I would never have imagined could be confirmed in the Bible. I have sat with Bible in hand asking for confirmation, saying something like, "I don't know how You're going to do this one." There have been times when I have questioned whether I am even to continue to do the work of my prayer and creative arts ministry. More than once, Holy Spirit has taken me to these verses, which have consistently been His way of telling me to stay the course and keep moving forward in art and ministry.

Do not neglect the spiritual gift within you, which was bestowed on you through prophetic utterance with the laying on of hands by the presbytery. Take pains with these things; be absorbed in them, so that your progress will be evident to all. Pay close attention to yourself and to your teaching; persevere in these things, for as you do this you will ensure salvation both for yourself and for those who hear you (1 Timothy 4:14–16, underlined emphasis mine).

Later, when God confirmed His call to expand my ministry into a department of a larger arts ministry organization, He took me to Judges 5.

"The peasantry ceased, they ceased in Israel,
Until I, Deborah, arose,
Until I arose, a mother in Israel"
(Judges 5:7, underlined emphasis mine).

"Awake, awake, Deborah;
Awake, awake, sing a song!"
(Judges 5:12, underlined emphasis mine).

The key phrase for me in these verses at the time was *"Until I, Deborah, arose, Until I arose."* What those words said to me was that God had given me a unique message that needed to be heard by others. It was and continues to be a message that only I can deliver. My time to "wake up" meant making my ministry official. By taking what I was already doing within my retail art studio and putting a formal organizational structure around it, I was committing to the **so much more** that God had for me. God used His word to specifically point me in a certain direction and confirm His leading. He never fails to confirm His word when it is His will for your life. Trust that He knows exactly how to get you to just the right verse in the Bible when you need it. Sometimes He uses other people to get you to the right verse. Other times, He uses other people to confirm His direction.

Witness of Others

Sharing what you have heard from the Lord with a few trusted advisors is always wise. Notice that I said trusted advisors. I did not say friends and family (although they could certainly be part of your sphere of trusted advisors). This action is one where not throwing your pearls before swine (Matthew 7:6) applies. I faced this hard truth personally a few years ago. I asked for prayer for something that the Lord had newly revealed for my future. I was excited and shared this directive with a group before I had inquired of the Lord. It was not the right time or group. I could almost feel the spiritual thud in the room. Later, in talking with one of my trusted advisors, we were able to discern a competitive spirit from within this group. It was not the right group to ask for confirmation; I had shared prematurely. Hold your revelation. Marinate in it before the Lord until such a time that

Holy Spirit says, *"This person and this time are safe."* He is faithful to you and to His call on your life. He will bring the right people to assist you.

Divine Appointments

It is amazing how quickly the Lord can bring just the right person into your life at just the right time. He will use other's needs and situations to give the instruction, *"This is the way, walk in it"* (Isaiah 30:21). I find that often a person I'm talking to will quote the very same verse I am camped on, confirming what God's telling me. Or, seemingly out of the blue, a person will ask me to do the very thing I felt the Lord leading me to do. That's the way of God. That's why we call them DIVINE appointments. They are orchestrated by Heaven.

We like to say it's a small world. I disagree. It is a great big, humongous world. We just serve a bigger God who can connect exactly the right people at the right time. Jesus told His disciples,

"Are not two sparrows sold for a cent? And yet not one of them will fall to the ground apart from your Father. But the very hairs of your head are all numbered" (Matthew 10: 29–31).

Dear One, you are loved and cared for by the One who created the universe. He created you for a purpose about which He cares deeply. He can and will align you with the right people at the right time to equip you and lead you to your destiny. His desire for your success is greater than your own. He created you to live a life of *so **much more**!* In addition to divine appointments, God creates divine opportunities to confirm His direction.

Opportunity

After a long "wilderness" season of no ministry several years ago, the spiritual atmosphere I was experiencing shifted. It began to feel as if the Lord was moving ministry from the back burner to the front burner of my life, but I knew nothing other than what I sensed in the Spirit. That wilderness season had taught me the much needed lesson of contentment, and I was concerned about running after something that wasn't in God's timing. I specifically asked the Lord to confirm the return to ministry. Within weeks, I was asked to speak, had several requests for personal appointments, and seemingly out of the blue, I was reconnected with others in ministry. Being offered opportunity is one way of confirming how and where the Lord wants to use your gifts. God uses other ways that may not be as obvious. He is creative and will often use very creative ways to underscore what you think, sense, or feel is the way He's leading. You may find Him speaking to you in the most unusual places and times.

Utterances

God may speak to you when you are looking for something to watch on TV and arbitrarily land on The Word channel. Listening to the speaker, you wonder if she has been walking alongside you listening in to the conversations of your heart. She seems to know exactly what you've been going through and need to hear from the Lord. That's God speaking and confirming His word!

Several years ago, I was inspired to paint a series of skies. Before I went in that direction, I asked the Lord to confirm it. The next Sunday morning, the opening line of a song reflected Psalm 19:1, "The heavens are telling of the glory of God." That was the Lord telling me that a painting series of skies could give Him glory as much as paintings based on His Word—it was my green light to move forward.

Signs, Songs, and Symbols

Natural things of the world become supernatural in the hands of the Lord when He chooses to use them to confirm His word. In my own life recently, He has used a paragraph from a science fiction novel, a song from a Broadway musical, and the name of a publishing house to speak to me. The Creator of the Universe has the world at His disposal and He uses it all. Specifically, I am referring to the written word and symbol here. Words and symbols do not have to be "religious" or from Scripture for the Lord to speak through them.

The author who writes the words that speak to you doesn't even have to be Christian. Are you familiar with the Christmas song "O Holy Night"? The story behind this song is quite amazing. It was first commissioned by a priest as a poem to be read. The author, Mr. Placide Cappeau, was not known to be a Christian. In fact, historically, he has been thought to be an atheist. He, in turn, asked his friend Adolphe Charles Adam to put the poem to music. Adam was of Jewish origin and faith. Together they penned a song that has inspired generations in spite of the fact that neither of them were Christian. The French church even banned the song because of the composer's lack of Christian faith. Creativity is a gift from God. He will use it for His plans and purposes—whether or not He is acknowledged in the process.

The long and unusual history of the distribution of this beloved song also points solely to the Lord. It was translated into English and brought to America by American abolitionist John Sullivan Dwight. The song then became a part of the legend of a 24-hour Christmas cease-fire in the Franco-Prussian War, and it was part of the first radio broadcast of a man's voice in 1906. As Dr. Jeff Sanders writes on his blog *A Moment in History*, "The song written by a wine merchant, set to music by a Jewish composer, banned by church leaders, kept alive by the French, adopted by American abolitionists, sung by troops in the trenches, and at last broadcast to the whole world by invisible radio waves. The first song ever played over the radio, 'O Holy Night'...Fall on your knees. O hear the angel voices. O night divine. The night when Christ was born. O night divine."[5]

The story of "O Holy Night" is a powerful example of God using any and everything on Earth to proclaim and confirm His wisdom, guidance, and direction for His children. He uses the natural realm and He uses supernatural experiences to show the way.

Supernatural Signs

God has innumerable ways to confirm His word. I have seen gold dust all over me—literally! Others could see it as well when I stepped out in faith to speak on something new. It happened during the last session of the first conference that I hosted at my home church. The Lord's Presence had been obvious during the entire conference. My prayer team had been praying for a physical manifestation of God's Presence for weeks before the conference started. We had even placed rain boots at the front of the sanctuary as a prophetic act, as if we were saying, "Lord, we are ready for you to show up!" I was sitting on my director's chair and paused a moment to collect my thoughts and ask the Lord for guidance. That's when I noticed that my skirt was full of what I can only describe as tiny glittery sparkles. It was as if Heaven had run gold through a sifter all over my clothes. Others ran to see it and some of them had gold dust on their hands and faces. It was a very tangible sign to me that God was with me, cheering me on. It was a sign to all who attended that Jesus—who walks on the streets of gold in Heaven—had walked among us. It remained on my clothing until well after I got home that evening. It has remained in my heart as one of the sweetest encounters I have ever had with the Presence of God.

I could fill this entire book with stories about the supernatural signs that God has shown to me and to others I know, but for brevity's sake, I will just point out a few more. Once I picked up a feather from the floor in a room where no feathers had been earlier. In that circumstance, I was unsure if I was taking the right step, and I desperately needed to know that the Lord agreed and approved of the direction that I was taking. Another time, the sweet fragrance of God was evident in the midst of a prayer session. In another instance, someone had oil suddenly appear on her hand as she looked at one of my paintings that depicts God's anointing being poured out on the world. As I recall these incidents, I see a common thread: God's children were open and even desperate to receive a sign of confirmation from Heaven that God was moving in these situations.

The take-away I want you to remember from these stories is that God is a supernatural God, and He will use supernatural signs to confirm His Presence and His direction. It may be unexplainable by the world's standards, but make no mistake about it, these signs exist and are from God. It bears repeating that the methods God uses to confirm His word and direction are as vast and varied as His children.

Fleeces and Lots

God's language is spiritual, mysterious, and supernatural. What else do you call it when there is dew on a fleece of wool and not on the floor, or on the floor but not on the fleece? In Judges 6:36–40, Gideon asked the Lord for a sign, directing where the dew should appear. Gideon was asking for confirmation, and the Lord lovingly responded to Gideon's request by doing exactly that. In New Testament times, the eleven disciples trusted God to reveal the replacement for Judas when they prayed before drawing lots.

"You, Lord, who know the hearts of all men, show which one of these two You have chosen" (Acts 1:24).

Does God still speak through fleeces and lots? Yes, I believe that He does! However, I will admonish you to handle these signs with care. The hearts of both Gideon and the disciples were in the right place at the time they asked for those kinds of specific signs.

These all with one mind were continually devoting themselves to prayer (Acts 1:14).

A devotion to prayer, humility, and faith are critical when using this type of confirmation. The types of confirmations I have given both in my personal examples and in the Bible are far from complete. They are meant to give a sampling of the many ways that God speaks and the multiple means that He has of confirming His word.

Rest, Trust, and Wait for More

God has a language all His own. A bluebird may mean nothing to me, but to someone else it is God's love language that says, *"Yes, you are in the right place."* Whatever method God chooses, He will confirm His word to you. You can be confident that you are hearing from Him in your life and as you complete the exercises in this book.

> *"For as the rain and the snow come down from heaven,*
> *And do not return there without watering the earth*
> *And making it bear and sprout,*
> *And furnishing seed to the sower and bread to the eater;*
> *So will My word be which goes forth from My mouth;*
> *It will not return to Me empty,*
> *Without accomplishing what I desire,*
> *And without succeeding* in the matter *for which I sent it"*
> (Isaiah 55:10–11).

These verses tell you that you can relax! You can rest in the Lord and trust that He will confirm whatever He wants you to know and do right now. One of the ways I knew it was time to write this book was that I had two speaking engagements cancel within five days of each other. They were the last speaking engagements I had for the year. I already had sensed the Lord was leaving the rest of my schedule clear so that I could focus on writing. Then a reservation for someone else to rent our condo in Florida was also cancelled, and a two-week window of opportunity suddenly opened before me.

It was my husband who first said, "You should go to our condo and take this time off to write your book." I was a bit stunned, nervous, and excited all at the same time. I knew he was right; God had made a way when there previously had been no way. He opens doors that no man can shut; He shuts doors that no man can open (Isaiah 22:22). These divine opportunities require your willingness to walk through the open door and to turn from a closed door to see where else He is leading you. I needed to say yes to God's direction and confirmation to experience the *so much more* that He had for me. In the process of writing and birthing this book, God has used a number of different ways to give me direction and confirmation. We still sometimes miss His direction—even with confirmations—so He gives them in multiple ways to get our attention.

Let me offer a word to the wise. Do not rely on just one of the ways that God confirms His direction. God is faithful to confirm His word. He will not let you miss it. He will make certain you have it right if you give Him the chance to do so. I am not naturally very good at this one, I will admit. As a visionary—translated dreamer—I want to run ahead and get started with whatever the Lord is speaking. I have learned my lesson and trained myself to allow the Lord to confirm His word through several methods. Give God the time to reveal His confirmations and to show you His timing in all that He reveals.

Giving God space and time to work is one of those push/pull areas of our Christian walk. On the one hand, we can heed the old saying, "fools often rush in where angels fear to tread." On the other hand, satan would love to derail your vision by turning your "waiting on the Lord" into paralysis, inertia, and complacency. Be mindful of both possibilities as you pursue what the Lord has for you. If you pause when He says pause, you are following your Audience of One, and you are being obedient to His directive.

Waiting on the Lord does not mean sitting on your hands until He drops the job offer, the singing gig, or the publishing contract into your lap. While you allow God's timing to unfold in your life, diligently pursue the Lord and activate the gifts placed within you. You will not be offered a job if you have never applied. You will not publish your book if you have never written anything. You will not be able to accept that singing gig if your vocal cords are out of shape. You will not be able to audition for that part if you have no "book"—the notebook of accompaniments that singers take to auditions. He will lead you with instructions about how to do your part during waiting seasons. In the same way that waiting doesn't mean don't do anything, working doesn't mean to do everything immediately when God releases the pause button and hits "play."

Don't Rush Ahead

Rushing into things can be detrimental to your future. Just this morning, I was given a vision of a closed door. In the first scenario, I ran towards that door. I stood before it impatiently waiting for it to open. In the second scenario, I walked towards the door, and, in the process, I met people who gave me gifts and encouraged my journey. When I reached the door, it opened to a sunlit path. The contrast between the scenarios was evident. I realized that, in the course of running, I had missed skills, opportunities, and people that would help my future. In my excitement to get to where the Lord was taking me, I cheated myself of blessings and relationships. There I stood, staring at the closed door, frustrated because it was not open. I heard the Lord say, "*When you take each step in My timing, when you allow Me to measure the length of your stride and the speed of your gait, not only do you reap the rewards and blessings I have for you along the way, but there is no time spent waiting at a closed door. You reach the door right as it opens.*"

There are times when the Lord will ask you to walk—like Jesus did. Consider all the lives that He touched as He did so: Zacchaeus (Luke 19:1–10), the woman at the well (John 4: 1–26), and the blind beggar (Luke 18:35–43) come to mind. Each of these was a life-changing encounter with Jesus the Messiah. None of these divine appointments would have occurred had Jesus not literally walked into His destiny one step at a time. Often God asks the same of you. He is figuratively saying: "*Walk don't run.*" The key is to focus on each day and take one step at a time, allowing the Lord to guide you. Yes, there are times when He will ask you to walk, but there are also times when He will ask you to run. It is wise to allow Adonai, your Teacher, to order your steps.

The mind of man plans his way, but the Lord directs his steps (Proverbs 16:9).

Within your heart, you can make plans for your future, But the Lord chooses the steps you take to get there (Proverbs 16:9, The Passion Project, TPT).

Allow the Lord to choose your steps. If you do not run ahead or strive to make things happen on your behalf, you are more prepared when God's doors open for you at the perfect time. My vision caused me to wonder how many times I have missed God's nuggets of truth and His blessings. I also may have created unnecessary tension in my life because I ran ahead of His perfect timing. Trust me, you will experience far less frustration and far more peace when you "actively" wait on the Lord's timing.

God's sense of timing is completely other-worldly. He sees everything from eternity's perspective. Psalm 90:4 says that a thousand years is like only a day to the Lord. That's eternal perspective! Obedience, faith, and surrender allow you to take one step at a time. The best way to live in the present moment, to stay on your path, and to let Jesus order your steps is by starting each day with the question, "What do You have for me to do today?" This inquiry from your heart allows the Lord to set the timetable for your journey. Once you know the "what," seek the "when" of God's plan, and watch more of your flight plan unfold.

Trust My Timing

About 20 years ago, my husband had interviewed for a new position that would cause us to move from the Dallas area to the Atlanta area. We had sought the Lord about this decision and felt strongly that we were to move. In fact, in a moment of true humility and faith, Rick had done the modern version of drawing lots and had tossed a coin. We totally believed the result that indicated we would be moving to Atlanta. Then it appeared as if the opportunity was being blocked because the corporate decision-makers were silent. One morning, as I was driving home from doing errands, I was crying out to the Lord. I was ready to move forward with the move. As clear as day, I heard the Lord speak to my spirit,

> *"Do you trust Me?"*
> **"Yes, Lord you know that I trust You."** I replied.
> *"Then trust My timing."*

To this day, hearing those words remains one of the times that I have heard the Lord the clearest. Hearing His words that clearly was all it took for me to learn the lesson of trusting God's timing. Within two weeks, Rick "accidentally" ran into a man who asked him if he wanted the job and who was in a position to make it happen, even though he was not in the normal chain of command. Two months later, we moved to Atlanta for the job.

I hear those words as clearly today as I did all those years ago. *"Then trust My timing."* It seems much easier to trust God for the path than to trust the speed at which you move along your path. God's timing is usually not our timing. Once you have heard the Lord, and He has confirmed His word, **go back and ask Him to confirm His timing.** I cannot stress this step enough. Remember that He looks at your life through the lens of eternity. Things look a little different from that perspective. Surrendering your future to Him means not only laying down your agenda items but also the order and timing of your plan as well. Confirmation brings confidence and certainty when the Lord says, *"Now is the time to step quickly, to run the race, to move forward* *in what I am telling you to do."* If you want more certainty, ask and wait for the Lord to confirm His word again.

It is now time for you to reflect on the "when" and "how" that you have seen the Lord confirm His word to you. Remembering is a way of giving honor and thanksgiving to the Lord for all that He has done in your life. It is a great habit to start. Exercises like the following are good to do periodically—not just as you read this book. As you remember, you make way for the Lord to act on your behalf again and again. Testifying to what Jesus has done in your life prophesies that He will do it in the future (Revelation 19:10). Let's take the time to remember, give thanks, and give God glory.

SOARING WITH GOD

Exercise 10: Confirmations

I want you to sit quietly with the Lord. Ask Him to show you the myriad ways that He has spoken and confirmed His word to you. Take out your notebook or journal. Divide your page into three columns.

1. In the first column, list the time/event of your remembrance.
2. In the second column, list the language the Lord used to speak to you about that event.
3. In the third column, list the way in which God confirmed His word or direction for you.

When I lead this exercise at conferences, I consistently hear surprise in people's voices as they recognize how faithful God is to confirm His word. They leave equipped with the confidence and *so much more* certainty that God will confirm every step in their journey—including the ones they currently face.

Exercise 11: Asking for Confirmation

God is faithful to direct and confirm His direction in your life. I know there are steps that you are facing right now. This chapter would not be complete if we didn't stop and ask the Lord to confirm what He is saying to you at the present time.

Turn the page in your notebook or journal. Once again, divide your page into three columns.

1. In the first column, list a directive that you have felt from the Lord.

2. In the second column, list how you came to know and understand this was a directive from the Lord. How did God reveal this to you? What language did He use?

3. Leave the third column blank.

4. Look over your list, and seek the Lord. Ask Him to confirm His directive and give you the timing to begin, work on, and finish what He has called you to do.

5. Over the next days, weeks, or months, keep this list before you, continuing to pray for those things not confirmed, and listing the confirmations in the third column as they occur.

You can be confident that **God is faithful to His children, His Word, and His direction**. You will receive confirmation, and with that confirmation, you will experience the *so much more* that the Lord has for you. He will give you more confidence and certainty in who you were created to be and in what you were created to do. That confidence and certainty is the experience of soaring with God!

CELEBRATING YOUR PROGRESS AND MOVING FORWARD

Hearing and confirming His word is exciting, isn't it? If you naturally like to move ahead quickly like I do, these chapters may have felt like a bit of a detour for you. After all, we didn't "do anything" that told you more of who you are or what you are meant to do. Seeking the Lord, tuning your spirit to hear, interpret, and confirm when He is speaking is foundational to the destiny journey that lies ahead. I promise you that these steps are valuable and absolutely necessary for moving forward in your destiny. Now that you have soared with God to strengthen your awareness and knowledge of hearing your Creator, you will live in *so much more* certainty when you hear His voice, whether it be through signs and symbols, emotions, or written word. Whatever way He chooses to speak and confirm His word, be certain that as you seek your Heavenly Father, He will reveal the *so much more* of who He created you to be. All that you have learned will be put to good use as we move forward to seek the Lord for your God-given identity.

Before we take the next step, let's take a minute to seal what we have learned about finding more certainty through confirmation in prayer.

Lord and Master, we thank You that You are faithful to never give up. You will always confirm what You are saying to Your children. Your ways are vast and beyond comprehension, but You love us enough to make sure we get the message. Bring greater certainty to Your children as they move forward in the *so **much more*** that You have for each and every one of them. In Jesus' name, Amen.

6.
Created For So Much More
IDENTITY:
Completing Your Passport

We each hear God on a unique frequency. You have a relationship and language with Father, Son, and Holy Spirit that is different from mine. To hear from the Lord, we must know who He is so that we recognize His voice. It is no less important for you to know who you are to establish a two-way conversation. Knowing who God says you are, and knowing your identity in Christ, is at the root of grasping the *so much more* that the Lord has for you.

In this day and age, if the Lord asked you to leave your country like He had done with Abraham in Genesis 12, one of the first things you might do is to check your passport to make sure it is valid and up-to-date. A passport is a record of who you are. It includes physical characteristics such as age, hair color, and eye color, as well as city, state, and country of residence. You know who you are, but a passport confirms to others that you are who you say you are.

Jesus knew who He was, but in Matthew's Gospel, He asked His disciples to tell Him who THEY thought He was. In Matthew 16, verses 1–4, we find Jesus admonishing the Pharisees and Sadducees—the religious leaders of the day—for not recognizing who He was, not even with the "signs" that followed Him and His preaching.

From verses 5–12, it seems that the disciples still do not understand who Jesus is. In the previous verses, Jesus spoke to the Pharisees and Sadducees about bad leaven, and the disciples think He is talking about bread. They ask themselves if Jesus is hungry. They have just experienced Jesus feeding more than 4,000 people with seven loaves of bread and a few small fish! Even after seeing such a miracle, the disciples seem stuck in the natural realm with their thinking.

From Matthew 16:13 to the end of the chapter, we find Jesus and the disciples in Caesarea Philippi. Allow me to give you a little history here. At this time, this town was the royal headquarters of Philip (Herod's brother). It had originally been named Caesarea after Caesar, but Herod's brother had added Philippi to elevate his own position and level of authority. Jesus has dealt with religious leaders who don't recognize who He is, He is surrounded by His own disciples who are still caught up in the natural world, and He finds Himself in a city where names mean something. Can't you just feel the teaching moment?

> *Now when Jesus came into the district of Caesarea Philippi, He was asking His disciples, "Who do people say that the Son of Man is?" And they said, "Some say John the Baptist; and others, Elijah; but still others, Jeremiah, or one of the prophets." He said to them, "But who do you say that I am?" Simon Peter answered, "You are the Christ, the Son of the living God." And Jesus said to him, "Blessed are you, Simon Barjona, because flesh and blood did not reveal this to you, but My Father who is in heaven"* (Matthew 16:13–17).

Jesus asks the question, "*Who do people say that the Son of Man is?*" (Matthew 16:13). Notice that He answers His own question within the question. The disciples were all of Jewish descent. They had all been raised hearing the teaching of the Old Testament prophets. When Jesus uses the phrase "Son of Man," He is giving a clue to the answer as told in the book of Daniel.

> *"I kept looking in the night visions,*
> *And behold, with the clouds of heaven*
> *One like a Son of Man was coming,*
> *And He came up to the Ancient of Days*
> *And was presented before Him.*
> *And to Him was given dominion,*
> *Glory and a kingdom,*
> *That all the peoples, nations and men of every language*
> *Might serve Him.*
> *His dominion is an everlasting dominion*
> *Which will not pass away;*
> *And His kingdom is one*
> *Which will not be destroyed"* (Daniel 7:13–14).

Did you catch the connection? Simon Peter has an aha moment. He connects Daniel's vision with Jesus, the Son of Man! In that moment, Simon Peter's answer switches from repeating what people were saying to speaking what is revealed to him from the Father. We could say that Peter switched from placing a label on Jesus to naming Him. Words like prophet or teacher represent what people do more than who they are. It is true that Jesus was a great prophet, a great teacher, and a healer, but those titles labeled him. In that moment of revelation, Simon Peter saw with Heaven's eyes. He saw beyond the labels of this world and saw the WHO of Jesus. He saw with Heaven's reality. He saw the "I AM" of Jesus (Exodus 4:14). He saw the *so much more* of Jesus.

Simon Peter's answer is a heart moment. His response, *"You are the Christ, the Son of the Living God"* (Matthew 16:16), implies more than labels or titles. It's as if his spirit is saying, "You are the Christ! You are the Anointed One! You are the promised Messiah!" You can feel Simon's passion in that moment of Heaven's revelation. In that moment of love and passion, Peter breaks out of the very labels that could have been pinned on him: "uneducated," "fisherman," "working class," and "follower." In contrast to those labels, Jesus prophesies.

"I also say to you that you are Peter, and upon this rock I will build My church; and the gates of Hades will not overpower it. I will give you the keys of the kingdom of heaven; and whatever you bind on earth shall have been bound in heaven, and whatever you loose on earth shall have been loosed in heaven" (Matthew 16:18–19).

Jesus then takes the moment of Peter's revelation and prophesies: *"You are Peter and upon this rock I will build My church* (Matthew 16:18). In that moment, Jesus confirms Peter's Heavenly identity. He speaks of the *so much more* of Peter: who he was created to be and what he was created to do. The world labels "fisherman," "uneducated," "working class." God names. God through Jesus says "Rock." "Leader." "Pillar of the faith." It is through Jesus' eyes and words that Peter glimpses into his future—the *so much more* of who he was created to be. It is through Jesus that you and I glimpse into our future and the *so much more* that we were created to be and do. It is the enemy, through the world around us, who builds the box that labels bring.

The World Labels; God Names

Make no mistake about it: satan, the father of lies, would like nothing more than for you to stay in the box that labels create. Boxes of education, profession, or roles you serve. The enemy would tell you that you are forever a product of your past. He wants you to be deceived into believing that your identity is based on what you do, how much money you make, where you live, or how big your sphere of influence is. These are all labels.

Labels are the enemy's boxes meant to keep you where you are. These labels are also strongholds that hold you back. They are chains that keep you captive, stymied, and unable to move forward in your journey. When you, like Peter, keep your spirit tuned to Heaven's perspective, you too break out of the labels that limit you. When you hear who the Lord says you are, you see yourself with new eyes. Jesus invites you to step out of those boxes and break free from the labels that hold you captive. Jesus invites you to see, hear, and understand the *so much more* of who you were created to be and the *so much more* of what you were created to do. Jesus holds out His hand and asks you to soar with Him.

Soaring with God on the journey of discovering the *so much more* of your identity and purpose can get messy. You must be willing to lay it all on the line to discover and accomplish all that the Lord is asking you to do. Not everything connected to your destiny and calling is fun or exciting. It takes work. Lots of it. Take responsibility for doing the work and move forward in what the Lord is revealing to you. The next exercise is powerful. For Julie, it was life-changing. She wrote, "God revealed and healed lies that I didn't even know were there!" There have been plenty of tears whenever I have presented this material. I find that those people who are most willing to go wherever the Spirit directs get the greatest revelation from the Lord. Don't miss that. Dig in. Go wherever the Lord wants to take you to show you the *so much more* of who He created you to be and what He created you to do.

SOARING WITH GOD

Exercise 12: Your Identity

I want you to carve out 15–30 minutes. Find a spot that is comfortable and relaxing. Choose some music that is soft and inspiring. I find that instrumental music works best. Involve your sense of taste with a cup of your favorite tea or coffee. Are you familiar with essential oils? Diffusing frankincense is wonderful for quieting the mind and creating a spiritual atmosphere. When I lead this exercise at my conferences, some participants have used my artwork as a visual centering point. If you have art that evokes your visual senses, feel free to gaze at it. Involving your senses as you prepare to meet the Lord gives Him a runway on which He can land. We find Him when we seek Him with all of our heart (Jeremiah 29:13), which is the center of all of our senses.

Take whatever time you need to ask the Lord these two questions AND allow Him space and time to answer. I find that approaching this as a journal exercise works beautifully. I pray that you will hear your Lord clearly as you meet and soar with Him during this time. **THIS EXERCISE HAS BEEN KNOWN TO BE LIFE-CHANGING! DO NOT SKIP IT TO GO ON TO THE NEXT SECTION!** Now is the time to sit quietly and ask the Lord these questions:

1. Lord, how much do You love me?
2. Father, Jesus, Holy Spirit, what were you thinking when You formed me in my mother's womb? (Psalm 139:13).

Take time to settle your spirit and write what comes to your mind. Think stream-of-consciousness. Trust that the Lord is meeting you in this moment. Allow Holy Spirit to whisper words or show you a picture. There is no right or wrong here! Listen to Holy Spirit. Write what you hear. Draw what you see. Trust that the Lord wants to speak to you today.

Once you have completed this exercise, I recommend staying put and pondering what the Lord has revealed to you. Even after that additional quiet time, it may be time to walk around and take a break to allow God's truth of who He created you to be to sink deeply into your heart, mind, and spirit.

Personal Brand/Message

What you have just done is the first step in developing a personal brand. We all have one. You might not run a business or ministry, but you still have a personal brand. How many times has a friend or family member said, "Oh, I saw something at the store you would love!" Or, perhaps they saw something when you were shopping together and said, "That looks just like you!" They are referring to your personal brand. You stand for something. That something is your brand. What I am doing here is raising your awareness of that something and giving it a name. What is the message your life speaks? Your actions should reflect your message wherever you go, whatever you do. It doesn't always work that way, however.

During the 26 years when my husband was in corporate life, we were surprised to learn that a number of his business associates, who often exhibited non-Christ-like behavior, regularly attended Christian churches. The first time we came across this discrepancy between professed belief and behavior, we committed to live in a manner that won't surprise others when they discover that we are Jesus Followers. In fact, I have found a good question to live by is, "Would others be surprised to hear that I am a Christ Follower?" The contrast between belief/message and behavior can be startling if your life doesn't exemplify Christ-like principles.

Not too long ago, I was stopped at a traffic light in the only lane that was marked to go straight. The left turn lane was to my left. The right turn lane was to my right. The light turned green, and the car to my right raced around me and cut me off. I had to chuckle as I read the license plate "I AM SECOND." What is "I am Second"? The organization's website says: "I am Second is a movement meant to inspire people of all kinds to live for God and for others."[6] In other words, God is first. "I am Second" may be the message of the movement, it was not the message of the driver I encountered. He was not living his message.

Exercise 13: Developing Your Life Message

What is your life message? What do you stand for? What do you want people to remember about you? This exercise is not about image. Image is based on labels. This exercise is about God's identity for you and the name/words He speaks over you—character words like faithful, trustworthy, authority, gifted, transparent, or authentic.

Go ahead. Take the time to jot a few words down. Add these to your answers from the previous exercise.

Live Your Message

Through this chapter and the exercises that you have completed, God has given you the *so much more* of who He created you to be. Your life message should reflect the identity that God gave you at birth and the character traits that He has honed and polished throughout your life. Your life message is like a billboard for all to see. Clothes don't make the man, but how you dress should reflect who you are as a Christ Follower and more. As an artist and director of a creative arts ministry, I would lose credibility if I showed up to speak to a group of artists dressed in a conservative buttoned-up suit and pumps. If as a minister of the Word of God, I wore anything that reflected anything other than Jesus is Lord, I would not be living my message. Therefore, I generally wear clothes that reflect my artistic nature and express my life as a Jesus Follower. What does that look like? You will often find me in long flowing skirts, with layers of tops or loose sweater-jackets, accessorized with jewelry or scarves that have been created by my artist friends. How you dress is a great visual for living your message, but living your message encompasses all aspects of your life.

How you treat others indicates what you stand for. What you say and how you say it matters when you are at the grocery store or in a business meeting. How you act and respond to others when you are driving or in line at an amusement park should reflect your life message. Living your message means allowing Holy Spirit to permeate all aspects of your life. Living authentically means being the person God created you to be.

You are already well on your way in your journey of discovering the *so much more* that the Lord has for you to discover. Navigators have known for centuries that you can find your way anywhere if you know which direction is "true north." Your "true north" for your destiny is your God-given identity. Within your identity are the keys that reveal your destination. Like the eagle, you soar with God when you fully accept and celebrate who He created you to be.

Hawks and eagles soar with little apparent effort. Their flight is not made up of flapping wings and striving to get from one place to the other. As I took my walk at a local soccer field one day, I was mesmerized by the sight of a hawk spiraling higher and higher on the air currents. I don't think I saw him flap his wings once as he gracefully moved along the sky soaring higher and higher. Holy Spirit whispered, *"See how little striving and effort there is when you let Me take you to new places?"* Soaring with God means resting in who He created you to be. As you rest in Him, He will provide the wind beneath your wings on which to spiral higher in Him and further in your destiny.

CELEBRATING YOUR PROGRESS AND MOVING FORWARD

Congratulations! You are completing your Heavenly passport! Unlike our Earthly passports, our Heavenly identity is never fully complete. God is always in process of refining us and pouring more of His identity into us. Although there is always *so much more* for God to reveal, you can be at peace with what you have today and who God says you are in the here and now. Our next step in this journey of discovery will give you the time and place to ask the Lord to expand your vision about your destiny—what He created you to do—as we take a look at the flight plan that He has for you.

Will you pray with me?

Heavenly Father, You are my Creator. I know that You form wonderful creations perfectly fit for a plan and purpose. Thank

You for who You created me to be. Thank You for revealing more of my identity as we soar together like the eagles. Lift me higher in You and further in my purpose and destiny as I continue to walk this journey with You. Send Your Holy Spirit to speak to my heart, mind, and spirit. In Jesus' name, I pray. Amen.

7.
Created For So Much More
VISION:
Designing Your Flight Plan

God created you to fly with vision and purpose. He designed you with exactly what you need to accomplish that purpose. You, however, are given free will. You can choose to wander purposelessly through life—or you can choose to plan and align your life choices with God's plan. Soaring with God to design your flight plan will bring a clearer picture—call it vision—for your future and the *so much more* that God has for you. So let's dive into the ideas and suggestions that help you co-labor with God to develop the plan that will empower your vision and enable your destiny.

In my work with creative people, I find there is an aversion to planning. Artists react even to words like plan, schedule, or goals. They feel as if I am asking them to wear a straitjacket while they are still trying to paint, write, play music, or dance. The truth is that a plan is important for you to soar with purpose. Our pilot must file a flight plan before takeoff; simply envisioning the destination will not get him there. All too often, people "take off" with a vision/directive/idea from the Lord only to crash and burn later. In most of those cases, no plan was in place to deal with the obstacles, resistance, and challenges encountered. Having a plan, seeing how things fit together, and seeking the Lord for order and direction keeps you from running ahead and running amuck.

Drawing up a flight plan begins by asking the Lord to reveal the *so much more* of what He created you to do. Asking for this revelation is not presumptive on your part. It astounds me how many believers seek a word of destiny from someone else, but they won't seek the Lord themselves for His plan and purpose for their lives. It seems people are comfortable seeking God for their identity, but they get squirmy when I tell them to ask the Lord to show them their destinies. Dear One, God invites you to sit at His feet and ask for His guidance for your future. Providing guidance is one of the reasons He sent the Holy Spirit.

"But when He, the Spirit of truth, comes, He will guide you into all the truth; for He will not speak on His own initiative, but whatever He hears, He will speak; and He will disclose to you what is to come" (John 16:13).

In this passage, Jesus is speaking. God the Son is telling His disciples what they can expect beyond His Ascension. He is teaching them about the Holy Spirit—the same Holy Spirit that is available to you and me. God, through the Holy Spirit, longs to speak to you. He wants to communicate what is to come. Communication is a two-way street. Yet, I have heard believers pray, "Lord, show me the way" and then fail to stop and listen for the Lord's answer. Take the time to seek the Lord for revelation for your flight plan **and then listen** as He speaks. You abide in the Lord. He abides in You (John 15:4). He will use your thoughts, notions, and dreams to speak His plan for this flight called life.

Your Unique Dream and Path

You carry ideas, pictures, visions, and dreams of your destiny—all of which are whispers from Heaven to help you discover your flight plan. Recently, I read that at some point during childhood, we all experience an open doorway where we catch a glimpse of our future. The world may not recognize that open doorway as a God moment, but we who follow Christ know it comes from Creator God. You may have lost sight of your God-given destiny, but it is still there. Take the time to search out the *so **much more*** of what you were created to do. Within the framework of who you are is the plan and purpose for which you were created. It may be obvious or hidden—but wherever or whatever it is, your flight path will look as unique as your framework.

You possess a gift mix and a personality profile that no one else has. You also have a unique flight path as you soar with God. No one else soars like you. No one shares your call. The Audience of One is the best navigator you can have. Trust the Lord's Word when He says,

Your ears will hear a word behind you, "This is the way, walk in it," whenever you turn to the right or to the left (Isaiah 30:21).

Hearing and understanding which way to turn is a significant promise from God. He will tell you which way to fly. I have personally experienced God's fulfillment of His promise of Him telling me which way to go on numerous occasions, but I'll share just one now.

It was a crossroads moment, and I was confused about where to take my art business. Overwhelmed with the choices and the voices offered by the world, I took the time to sit with the Lord and seek His direction. As I pondered with Holy Spirit, I saw myself walking in a dense jungle. The jungle was dimly lit, yet the underbrush was as thick as the canopy. The image epitomized how I felt: blinded, disoriented, and confused. Stymied by so many choices, I could not move. Jesus appeared in my jungle and began walking in front of me, machete in hand. He cut through the limbs that threatened to hinder my progress, and I found myself stepping solidly in the direction that He was leading. I heard His whisper, "*I am your Trail Blazer. Go where I tell you. Do not look at other artists' paths; follow Me and My path for you.*" I picked up pen and paper, and did one of the exercises included in this chapter. He then brought clarity and revelation for the decisions that I needed to make for my business.

I liken this vision of Jesus as Trail Blazer to the navigator that sits in the cockpit of a jetliner. Pilots rely on the navigator to make sure that the way is clear, to redirect the path through any storms, and to keep the plane heading in the right direction. It is the navigator who ensures that the plane lands at the correct destination. Jesus is your Navigator. As you soar with Him, He knows the way and has a flight plan that fits perfectly with your life and your call. His flight path will ensure that you arrive at your God-given destination because He knows you and the best way to go.

Known, Chosen, with a Purpose

In the last chapter, we established that you are known by God. We have also established that you have a unique purpose. What if your purpose and destiny have already happened? All you would need to do is take possession of what has already happened and apply it to your daily life. In other words, your job would be to appropriate what has already taken place in the spiritual realm and apply it to the natural realm—the circumstances in your life. Does that idea sound a bit preposterous and even heretical to you? I admit that I wrestled with God over this concept, but it is a biblically-based insight, and it offers a fresh perspective that brought me closer to Him.

Let's take a look at a few key Scriptures with this idea in mind.

"Before I formed you in the womb I knew you, and before you were born I consecrated you; I have appointed you a prophet to the nations" (Jeremiah 1:5, underlined emphasis mine).

Before God formed Jeremiah, He knew him and his purpose. God also knew you before you were born. **God knew His plan for you and set you apart for that purpose before He formed you.** Your Creator knew you spiritually before you became manifest physically on Earth. Here are a few more Scripture nuggets to chew on.

We have become His poetry, a recreated people that will fulfill the destiny He has given each of us, for we are joined to Jesus, the Anointed One. Even before we were born, God planned in advance our destiny and the good works we would do to fulfill it! (Ephesians 2:10, The Passion Translation, TPT, underlined emphasis mine).

And in your book were all written {past tense} the days that were ordained for me, when as yet there was not one of them (Psalm 139:16, underlined emphasis mine).

All who dwell on the earth will worship him, everyone whose name has not been written from the foundation of the world in the book of the Lamb who has been slain (Revelation 13:8, underlined emphasis mine).

Just as He chose us in Him before the foundation of the world, that we would be holy and blameless before Him. In love He predestined us to adoption as sons through Jesus Christ to Himself, according to the kind intention of His will (Ephesians 1:4–5, underlined emphasis mine).

Each of these Scriptures points to an idea and indeed a mystery indicating that God has known us and our purposes since before time began. I must admit that, for the most part, I have previously viewed these types of verses as nice poetic language. My interpretation of the poetic language was, "Isn't that nice that the Lord knows me so well." Now I think there is more to this concept. What if the idea of being known and consecrated for a purpose before being formed is not sweet poetic language? What if our days really were ordained before we were born? What if God's plan for your life was in place before the foundations of the world were formed? We say that God knows the end from the beginning. What if that principle is not just God flexing His omniscient muscle, but in fact the end has already happened in the spirit realm? Our task becomes accessing on Earth what has already happened in Heaven. Isn't that what we pray in the Lord's Prayer when we say *"Thy kingdom come. Thy will be done in earth as it is in heaven?"* (Matthew 6:10, KJV, underlined emphasis mine). "As it is" means it already exists in Heaven! Scripture is full of other references to support the idea that the reality we experience in the natural or Earthly realm already exists in the supernatural or Heavenly realm. Here is just one:

> *For those of us who believe, faith activates the promise and we experience the realm of confident rest! For he has said,*
> **"I was grieved with them and made a solemn oath,**
> **They will never enter into the calming rest of my Spirit."**
> *God's works have all been completed from the foundation of the world for it says in the Scriptures,*
> **"And on the seventh day God rested from all His works"**
> (Hebrews 4:3–4. The Passion Translation, TPT, underlined emphasis mine).

God's works have all been completed from the foundation of the world! The writer of Hebrews quotes Genesis 2:2, which states that God rested on the seventh day *"from ALL His works"* ("ALL" capitalized emphasis mine). All means all. If God knew us and our purpose before the beginning of time, we should dig deeper and ask about the foundation of the world. We should ask: "When was it set in place?" "When was the beginning?"

Where can we read about time "before the foundations of the world?" Where can we explore the beginning? Let's go to the front of the book—the first book of the Bible.

> *In the beginning God created the heavens and the earth.*
> *The earth was formless and void, and darkness was over the surface of the deep, and the Spirit of God was moving over the surface of the waters.*
> *Then God said, "Let there be light"; and there was light* (Genesis 1:1–3).

To truly understand this passage, we need to look at the original language and decipher what is behind the English version that we know so well. Understanding Hebrew is an arduous task. The written Hebrew language contains layers of meaning behind every word. Each letter of the Hebrew alphabet is as much pictogram as it is a letter that forms a word. Those who study the language consider that picture in addition to the word and the whole sentence to accurately interpret the written language. Additionally, each letter of the alphabet carries a numeric, literal, and symbolic meaning. I am not a Hebrew scholar. Shane Willard is. He is a full-time minister who runs an international ministry (Shanewillardministries.org). His credentials and experience include being mentored by a pastor who had rabbinical training and teaching the context of the Scriptures from a Hebraic perspective.

In his sermon series, *Positioned to Win*, Mr. Willard translates the pictures and words of the Hebrew language in Genesis 1:1–3 and presents this summary statement: "In the beginning God, Jesus the Messiah, created the Heavens and the Earth. And the Earth became crazy and the craziness invaded your house because you did not have a revelation of the covenant of the nail. This led your life to a continual pattern of disrepair because the boundaries you chose were consuming your covering. This life of disrepair was presenting itself in the face of God's hidden blessings so God responded to this slap in the face by relaxing and declaring a solution full of grace and truth. A Word that was both with Him and was Him. Let the One who is Light shine."[7]

In other words, the Hebrew language and symbols of these first passages of Scripture suggest that Christ's death and Resurrection happened before Genesis 1:1–3! Genesis 1:4 and the rest of the Bible record a physical manifestation of what had already happened in the spiritual realm! That's quite astonishing to think about.

I will admit this revelation of future natural events having already happened in the spiritual realm has caused a major paradigm shift for me. What I am about to say is simply one way to look at things. At times, interpreting biblical language is like dealing with prophetic language, vision, and dreams. This interpretation is more art than science. Like an artist who carries a unique world view, I offer my view and application of this idea. I am not saying this perspective of events already happening in the spiritual realm is the only way to see things, but I must admit the eyes of my heart have been opened to see the possibility. What if my life has already been played out in the spiritual realm and I am living the physical manifestation here on Earth?

What if the movie of your life has already been produced? What if it simply hasn't been completely released to the theater of your life? What if when you get a glimpse of the future, when you capture and hold on to an image the Lord has given you, when you prophesy over your life, or when you receive a prophetic word from someone else, you are seeing, speaking, and experiencing the trailer for this movie of your future? Why does it matter?

So What?

I admit this paradigm shift has changed how I think about the dreams and visions I carry. I see them more literally as pictures of what I believe the Lord has in store for me. For instance, I am sitting on the balcony at our condo in Florida during a two-week retreat orchestrated by the Lord for me to get away from distractions and write this book. I have carried a picture of me doing just this kind of activity from the day we bought this condo three-and-a-half years ago. That prophetic picture was planted in my heart by Holy Spirit. He gave me a peek at the trailer of my future.

How you approach each day would change if your movie is already "in the can," wouldn't it? Rather than working endlessly to conjure up your destiny, you would simply need to access it from Heaven! It is a game-changer when it comes to how you feel about your future and how you live each day carrying the hopes, dreams, and visions of your future destiny. Trust replaces worry. Confidence replaces doubt. The voice of the Lord—who knows the end from the beginning—more easily overtakes the voices of doubt that come from the Greek chorus you hear. The voice of God—the producer of your life's movie—silences the enemy of our soul's whispers, which threaten to derail you.

Beyond more trust, confidence, and clarity, what difference would it make for you to appropriate what has already happened into your daily life? You could relinquish control and stop trying to figure it all out. Instead of striving to accomplish your dreams, you could rest, live in the moment, and take the step put before you this day. Remember the eagle who soars while gliding? You too could soar with God while gliding on His directions and currents. You could soar with God and not grow weary.

Yet those who wait for the LORD will gain new strength; they will mount up with wings like eagles, they will run and not get tired, they will walk and not become weary (Isaiah 40:31).

You don't need to muster strength or power, but rather, you could allow the Spirit to move on your behalf.

'Not by might, nor by power, but by My Spirit,' says the LORD of hosts (Zechariah 4:6).

You could be still and let God be Lord of your life.

"Cease striving *and know that I am God"* (Psalm 46:10).

When you loosen your grip on the future and cease striving to accomplish your vision for your future in your own strength, you open your hand to receive the *so much more* of God and what He has for you. You are available to see, hear, and accept what God has for you today. As I have said before, walk, don't run as you glimpse into your future, dream with God, and grab hold of your identity, your purpose, and your destiny. You will gain *so much more* joy, peace, and contentment if you stay present and simply do what He asks of you today.

Martin Luther is credited with saying, "Even if I knew that tomorrow the world would go to pieces, I would still plant my apple tree."[8] Apparently planting that tree was on his to-do list for the day. Controversy exists about whether or not Martin Luther actually said this, but the truth holds. This example is a great picture of living in the moment and letting God take care of the future.

You can rest in the notion that your future has already been determined. You "live now" when you walk each day in faith that God has your future in His hand and on His radar. The frustration of seeing and experiencing the disparity between your now and your future dreams turns to joy as you allow God to be God. Fully embracing the present ignites the passion to live a life fully engaged with God's plan and purpose. Don't be surprised when He shows you big things—that's His way!

Dream Big

God is a big God. He has big audacious plans for His children. It is often said that if you can accomplish your vision in your own strength, it is not God's vision. His plan for you is often much bigger than you can possibly see. Picasso said, "Every child is an artist. The problem is how to remain an artist once he grows up."[9] Like the artist child, the dreams we have as children often become buried in the responsibilities of adult life. So, if that picture in your heart seems like childish ambition, unrealistic, or too big to be true—it's not! God is showing you the future! Dream big and carry it with the childlike faith that God requires to accomplish it.

To inspire you to carry your childlike faith and big visions close to you, I'd like to share an excerpt of a song that touched me so much that I immediately asked for the lyrics when I heard it. It was written by my good friend Jim Gamble, who is a singer, songwriter, and storyteller for the Lord. You can learn more about Jim from his website (Jimgamblestoryteller.com).

"Wendy's Kitchen"

When Wendy had been moved ten times—once for each year she'd lived,
She had choices—to become bitter—to hide—or to give,
but in her heart she saw a future where she had her own home,
How? Or When?—she didn't know, but she knew it would come.

So through the years she kept the vision her eyes didn't see,
of a home with Wendy's kitchen—and what it would be!

Wendy's Kitchen is a wonder to see,
she's got pots and pans, she's got wine and cheese,
she's got cats, and coffee mugs, artwork, and grease,
Wendy's Kitchen is a wonder to me.

One husband, two daughters, three cats, and a yard,
all blessed by Wendy's gifts—and the kindness of God.
Still, her story doesn't end here, it's told far and wide.
to keep hope and nurture visions you see deep inside!

'Cause Wendy's Kitchen is a wonder to see,
she's got pots and pans, she's got wine and cheese,
she's got cats, and coffee mugs, artwork, and grease,
Wendy's Kitchen is a wonder to me."[10]

What a wonderful story of a child holding on to her God-given big dream and allowing Him to bring it to pass! It is also a story of how a big dream can bring hope to others when it is given to God to accomplish. It is good to dream big dreams! Don't negate big dreams just because they don't seem possible when you look at your circumstances.

Perhaps you have a big dream, but you see other people doing something similar and think that means that you're not meant to accomplish your dream. You may be in a profession or calling that looks and feels similar to others. The word similar is interesting. According to *The American Heritage Dictionary of the English Language*, it means "related in appearance or nature; alike though not identical."[11] You may have a SIMILAR profession or calling—but no one has an IDENTICAL profession or calling. The Lord brought this message home to me a few years ago as I prepared for one of my first conferences.

The Lord asked me to host a conference about prophecy. This endeavor was a first for me, and I wanted to prove myself worthy of the call, so I gathered all of my books by the "greats" to study. As I began to read, inferiority nipped at my heels. I couldn't see how I measured up to those "greats," and I began to question the assignment. It was then that I heard the Lord's whisper, *"Close the books. Put them away. Speak what I have taught you."* You and I don't have to be "great." We need to be obedient to the path the Lord has for us—even if it seems like we are tracing someone else's path, we are not. We each have our own voice, purpose, and path.

Within and outside of the Christian sphere of influence, myriad books are published on purpose and destiny. At times, I have questioned God's reasons behind this book. Each time I bring this question before Him, the Lord faithfully shows me that I have a unique message, because I have a unique experience and background. I am writing this book because He asked me to. Obeying the unction and mandate of Holy Spirit without thought to comparison is critical. To compare leads to despair. You alone carry the mantle given to you by your Creator to be the best YOU in the world.

Seth Godin is a well-known marketing guru and *New York Times* best-selling author. In his book *The Dip*, he speaks of being the "best in the world." He explains this phrase as, "Best as in: best for them (your audience) right now, based on what they believe and what they know. And in the world as in: their world, the world they have access to."[12] You, Dear One, were created to transform the world where you live. By soaring with God in who He created you to be and what He created you to do, you are transformed into the best YOU in the whole world, which is exactly what you need to change the world.

You don't have to change jobs or move to Africa to change the world. You can be nine or 90 years old, be male or female, have multiple degrees or not. You were designed and created to change the world here and now, where you are, and where God will take you. Your flight plan will look completely different from anyone else's. Only you soar on your flight path.

I am not suggesting that you are an island and without the need of other people on your journey. What I am saying is that no matter how closely you walk with others, you alone are responsible for what God has created you to do. I am on a solitary retreat as I write this book. My husband couldn't be more supportive of all that the Lord has asked of me. Rick is right there by my side as my single greatest supporter. But, we recognize that I am the one that walks out this ministry mandate. He doesn't go with me every time I speak. He is not in the room whenever I am giving prophetic counsel or walking someone through inner healing. Those are my assignments, which I alone carry. Likewise, you are solely responsible, in the Lord's strength, to do what the Lord is asking of you. You alone are given the privilege of walking the path of your life.

Certainly, there are times when our life path follows where others have gone. Other times, the Lord will ask you to go where no one you know has traveled. Ralph Waldo Emerson once said, "Do not go where the path may lead. Go instead where there is no path and leave a trail."[13] With Jesus as your Trail Blazer, you may indeed go where there is no path and leave a trail for others to follow. Allow Jesus to plan your flight, and you will find yourself soaring in a new direction in the midst of an adventure like none other. Wherever you soar, you can trust the result and impact to God. He alone sees the big picture and understands how all of our flight plans fit together for Kingdom impact. **As a Christ Follower, you should be more concerned with Kingdom impact than worldly impact.** The two kinds of impact can look different and are measured differently.

Your purpose in the Kingdom is not measured by how much you impact the world. Nor is your purpose measured by how many downloads your songs have, how much money you make, where you live or shop, or how well-known you are. In other words, your purpose is not related to the effectiveness scale of the world. The steps that the Lord asks you to take may not seem like giant steps, but He sees the Kingdom effect of your journey. Let's take a look at Peter's path to gain a better understanding of Kingdom purpose and impact.

Peter's Path

Jesus prophesied Peter's church leadership when he said, *"You are Peter, and upon this rock I will build My church"* (Matthew 16:18). As a man who had spent his life as a fisherman, being called the Rock that would support Christ's church must have seemed like a pretty big and audacious vision for Peter. A story in the last chapter of the Gospel of John after the Resurrection and before the Ascension and Pentecost, brings insight to the flight path Jesus had in mind for Peter. The passage gives a hint to God's heart for Kingdom purpose and impact.

> *So when they had finished breakfast, Jesus said to Simon Peter, "Simon, son of John, do you love Me more than these?" He said to Him, "Yes, Lord; You know that I love you." He said to him, "Tend my lambs." He said to him again a second time, "Simon, son of John, do you love Me?" He said to Him, "Yes, Lord; You know that I love you." He said to him, "Shepherd My sheep." He said to him the third time, "Simon, son of John, do you love Me?" Peter was grieved because He said to him the third time, "Do you love Me?" And he said to Him, "Lord, You know all things; You know that I love you." Jesus said to him, "Tend My sheep"* (John 21:15–17).

We could spend the rest of the book studying the intricacies of this passage and the meaning of the words. What I want us to focus on is the flight plan that Jesus is revealing to Peter. What are Jesus' instructions for this "Rock" who would become a pillar of the church? *"Tend My lambs." "Shepherd My sheep." "Tend my Sheep."* Some translations use *"Feed My sheep"* all three times. Tending sheep is not a lofty profession. Being a shepherd is lonely, dangerous, and dirty. Shepherds were not high on the totem pole of society. What Jesus is asking of Peter—the pillar and leader of the church—is to serve.

The singular and the plural version of sheep is the same word. Sheep. By saying, *"Feed My sheep,"* Jesus is not distinguishing the size of the call. He is not making the distinction between a single sheep or a flock of sheep. It makes no difference to the Lord how many people are being served. In the parable of the lost sheep (Luke 15:1–7), Jesus explains that there is more joy in Heaven over one sinner who repents than over 99 who need no repentance. Whether the sheep are singular or plural, Jesus asks Peter to do the work of serving, feeding, and tending those who the Lord brings, without consideration of fame or results. In essence, Jesus is asking Peter to take one step at a time, trusting that these steps of serving one sheep, or many, would lead him into his destiny as a leader.

Like Peter, your purpose is not related to results. Results are God's job. Your job is to listen when the Lord says, *"This is the way, walk in it"* (Isaiah

30:21). Your job is to follow your flight path wherever, whenever, and however He shows it to you.

SOARING WITH GOD

It is up to you to take the time to be quiet before the Lord to learn about His plans, purposes, and directions for your life. The world calls it daydreaming, envisioning, or brainstorming. I call it Cloud Forming.

Exercise 14: Cloud Forming

Many have reported this exercise to be a useful life tool. It may feel a bit uncomfortable at first, but stick with it. It will be incredibly helpful to propel you forward in your journey with the Lord. In essence, you are interpreting revelation from Heaven into diagram form. I call it Cloud Forming because you will be "blue-skying it" with the Lord, which means seeking Heaven's perspective for your life.

Sit quietly with music, a cup of tea, and perhaps essential oil diffusing into your atmosphere. Do whatever helps unlock your spirit to receive from the Holy Spirit. Tune in and wait. Allow Holy Spirit to lead you into His plan and purpose for your life and future. Sit, listen, and write what you hear.

One of the most intimidating moments I face as an author is to stare at a blank piece of paper wondering what to write. It is less intimidating to begin where I have left off. To help you over this intimidating hurdle, you are going to use Exercise 12 from Chapter 6 as your starting point. This cloud formation will be based on your unique qualities. Who God created you to be, where you live, and even how old you are, are characteristics that can shed light on your purpose and God's flight plan for your life. We are going to use what you heard Holy Spirit say when you asked Him what He was thinking when He created you. Who did He create you to be? Here we go! Are you ready to soar with God?

There is no right or wrong in this exercise. Your cloud formation, like you, will be unique.

Step 1: In the center of your page write your name.
Step 2: Form circles around your name with the interests, talents, or gifts that the Lord spoke to you.

Next we will expand your cloud to include who God said you are. These circles/bubbles/clouds create your unique cloud formation. Within each bubble, write a different characteristic, talent, or gift spoken to you earlier. For instance, you might write mother, father, son, daughter, teacher, artist, Jesus Follower, servant, communicator, healer, leader, caregiver, intercessor, etc., around your name. Think broad-brush strokes. For example, during this exercise, the Lord told Susan that He created her to be a mother, teacher, Jesus Follower, leader, and artist. Her cloud formation looks like this.

Cloud Forming
Steps 1 & 2

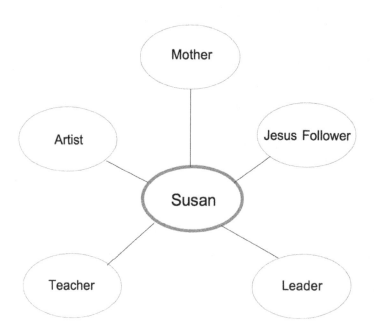

Step 3: Take each one of those bubbles and drill down a bit.
This time, be more specific. Ask yourself questions like: As a teacher, do I love to teach large or small groups? Am I inspired to teach a particular age group or gender? What subject matter ignites a fire within me? Where do I envision myself teaching?

Remember, we are still asking the Lord to show you who you are. Using each of the answers to those questions, fill another bubble in your formation. Think of these bubbles like spokes of a wheel coming out from the larger bubble. Susan's bubbles are Spanish (subject), youth (age group), underprivileged (group) in that area of who she is. You can see that Susan also added art to the area of teacher, perhaps as a vehicle by which she can teach Spanish. She also knows that she prefers to teach in a classroom rather than one-on-one tutoring. Each of these are things that she feels passionately about. Let me reiterate. This exercise is not what you currently do, **it is about who you are**, what you are passionate about, your gifts and talents, and how God sees you.

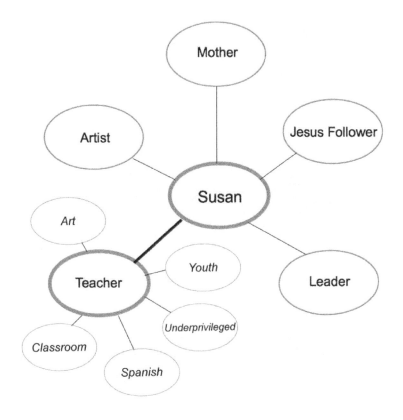

Cloud Forming
Step 3

I find that's about as deep as I can go on one piece of paper. At this point, you have put in diagram/cloud form what the Lord spoke earlier about who you are as you completed your passport. He may have also given you more details as you did this diagram. That's wonderful. Sit and study your cloud formation. Ponder what the Lord revealed and celebrate who He created you to be. I am thrilled for you! I am proud of you! You have heard your Audience of One and you are realizing more of your identity—who He created you to be. Congratulations!

Now it's time to go beyond your identity to grasp the *so much more* of what God created you to do. We know that you were created for a purpose. We know that God placed your purpose within the very characteristics and talents that you possess. We are going to use your newly-created cloud formation as a treasure map to unearth God's purpose and plan.

Exercise 15: Establishing Your Flight Plan

Your flight plan is God's vision, plan, and purpose for your future. In an earlier exercise, you asked God who He says that you are. The question you will be asking Him here is, "Where am I going?" **You must know where you are before you can plan where you are going.** That's why I want you to begin with your last cloud formation. This time, you will take **one aspect** of your identity and seek the Lord for His purposes attached to that aspect. I would suggest that as you begin this cloud formation, you take the time to ask Holy Spirit which bubble He is highlighting for you at this time. In our example, we will use Susan's teaching characteristic.

Take one of your main bubbles from Step 2. Place it in the center of a fresh piece of paper.

Now is the time to flesh out specifics and add the details you already know, or ask the Lord for fresh revelation about this area of your life. Ask the Lord, "What are Your plans for me?", "Where are You leading me?", and "How do You want me to use these gifts, talents, and characteristics?" Again, allow Him to flow through your thoughts.

Exercise 16: Expanding Your Flight Plan

You can see from the cloud forming diagram labeled Susan's Flight Plan that she has "blue-skyed" with the Lord about an after school program. She has expanded her possible subjects, recorded thoughts about potential locations, and added administrative things like scheduling, marketing, and registration.

Cloud Forming
Susan's Flight Plan

Now it's your turn. **Write everything down.** This is not the time to edit. In essence, **you are brainstorming with Holy Spirit.** There are no right or wrong answers. This exercise is not meant to be analytical or logical. Just let it flow—remember you are "blue-skying it" with the Lord. He may surprise you. I often receive huge revelation about projects and areas of my life when I take the time to process with the Lord this way.

How does your cloud formation look? If you find that your page is getting a little too one-sided and you are running out of room, it is time to take one of those bubbles and start a new page. This method is a great way to think through projects and ideas. It is what I did before I ever sat down at my computer to write this book. Many authors use outlines to map a book; I mapped out the material used in my conferences to mesh the messages into one cohesive package as a cloud formation.

Use the Cloud Forming exercise every time you sense Holy Spirit leading you into something new. It will give you a flight plan to follow from one place to another. Beginning the process may remind you of your first time travelling by air. You may get butterflies and feel the excitement of a future soaring with God. Cloud Forming is a tried-and-true process. Trust the method. Trust the Lord's desire to speak to you, and ask Him to share His plan with you.

Exercise 17: Determining Specific Flight Plan Takeaways

Now I want you to do me a favor. Sit awhile with your pages of cloud formations. Continue to ask the Lord to highlight areas. Are there areas you've been neglecting? Take a fresh piece of paper and write them down. I hear so many artists say that they have forgotten how much they enjoy painting because they hadn't tended their gift! Maybe God wants to bring something to the forefront that has been on the back burner. Perhaps you see new areas that need to be explored and developed. God is faithful to your purpose and your flight path. He will direct your thoughts. **Make a list of those areas that Holy Spirit is highlighting to you.** Keep it available, because we will add to it soon, and use it in the next chapter.

Just as clouds take on different shapes and colors from one moment to the next, so do the cloud formations that develop from this exercise. Every time you engage in Cloud Forming, your page will look a little different. What the Lord gives you today may just be a stepping stone for tomorrow's dream. Our flight plans are always in a state of flux. You may reach one destination, explore it for a while, and then realize the Lord has another path and place for you to travel.

The Adventure of Life

The adventure of life following Jesus is much more of a roller coaster than a merry-go-round. I have never found my life to be boring when I have surrendered my plans to the Lord and let Him plot my course. Being vulnerable before the Lord is key to moving forward in what He is asking you to do. There may be some big leaps before you. Julia Cameron, in her book *The Artist's Way*, teaches us to leap, trusting that the net will appear.[14] I agree, but in this adventure with the Lord, I have found that He often says *"Leap, and I'll give you wings to fly."* Staying connected with the Lord is how you will know whether it is time to take a leap or time to be still. Either can be risky in this world. He will equip you with whatever is needed at the time. Besides showing you the risks ahead, your cloud formation is an excellent indicator of skills that may be lacking if you are to accomplish your big dream. Take a good look at your cloud formation. Now take a good look at your life. See any discrepancies? There's your area to work on.

Just because you are gifted or talented at something doesn't mean you can't improve. Do not be afraid to edit your skills, rewrite your script, or do the work to improve your area of expertise. In this world of computer technology, educational resources are just a click away. Perhaps it is time for one-on-one training, coaching, or mentoring. Do not grow complacent. Practice. Rehearse. Write and rewrite. Take what is good and work to make it remarkable. Seth Godin in his book *Purple Cow*, says that the opposite of remarkable is very good.[15] Think about that a moment. The danger of being very good is that it is easy to accept things just the way they are. The difference between very good and remarkable is taking risks and honing skills. You could be an opening act—or you could be a headliner. It may take some work. It certainly takes being brutally honest with yourself and your current skill level.

Take a good look at your cloud formation with an objective and critical eye. **Ask yourself which areas need honing**. Add them to your list from Exercise 17. Learning a new or necessary skill may take you out of your comfort zone. Hallelujah! God has put His finger on a new area of exploration for you and He will meet you in that journey. Don't avoid those areas, or you may miss the excitement that God has for you.

As T.D. Jakes writes in his book *Destiny*, "Those who avoid the lure of creativity are residents of the comfort zone. Those who like safety inhabit the comfort zone. The comfort zone is the land of the status quo whose language is, 'We've never done it that way before.' Those words stop progress, stifle creativity, and halt innovation. Life in the comfort zone requires no challenge, no guts, and no determination."[16] I would add that no risk, adventure, or excitement is required in the comfort zone. Take responsibility for your skill set. Do the work necessary to improve the gifts and talents that you were given to enable you to do what you were created to do.

I hope you wrote out some big audacious dreams! I believe that God makes our dreams bigger than our abilities so that we must lean on Him and rely on Him. His Word says that in our weakness He is made strong (2 Corinthians 12:9). He prefers us to be reliant on Him—not self-reliant. Big dreams require us to lean on Him for wisdom, guidance, strength, and courage.

Joshua

The first chapter of Joshua has always held incredible significance for me. I cannot tell you how many times the Lord has led me to this amazing book. As the story opens, Joshua is faced with filling Moses' shoes. I can only imagine how intimidating that must have been. Between the end of the Book of Deuteronomy and the beginning of the Book of Joshua, the Israelites have arrived at the banks of the Jordan River. They are on the edge of the Promised Land that they have been pursuing for 40 years in the wilderness. It falls to Joshua to lead them over the Jordan River into Canaan. The weight on Joshua's shoulders must have been immense. What does the Lord say to this newly-appointed, inexperienced leader of His Chosen People?

"Just as I have been with Moses, I will be with you" (Joshua 1:5).

The first thing God does is promise to be with Joshua just as He had been with Moses. Those words must have been such a comfort to Joshua! Then, in Joshua 1:6, 7, and 9, the Lord repeats the phrase, *"Be strong and courageous"* to Joshua three times, including one that says, *"Only be very strong and very courageous."* Think about how much Joshua must have needed to hear those words for the Lord to repeat them three times! Think of how often you have needed to hear the Lord say the same thing: *"Be strong and courageous."*

Recently when I was camped in Joshua 1, Holy Spirit highlighted and underscored verse 3,

> *"Every place on which the sole of your foot treads, I <u>have given</u> it to you, just as I spoke to Moses"* (Joshua 1:3, underlined emphasis mine).

By using the words *"have given,"* the Lord is describing something that began happening in the past that also speaks of a future event. Grammatically, this use of the present perfect tense perfectly describes God's hand in the past and present for the benefit of the future. The use of the present perfect tense shows that He had already begun to go before Joshua and was giving him the land. I have combined the truth of the Joshua verses to help me through uncertain times. It is comforting to know that the Lord goes before me. It brings confidence to remind myself that He is my source of strength and courage. My paraphrase becomes: "Be strong and courageous for I have given you the land."

SOARING WITH GOD
Exercise 18: Be Strong and Courageous
Now we are going to use my paraphrase from the first chapter of Joshua as the basis of our next exercise. It is designed to connect this truth with the cloud you have formed and the big dream you carry within your spirit.

Take the time to settle in with the Lord and let Him finish each sentence as you work through that paraphrased truth.

Fill in the blanks as you are led by the Lord. Let Holy Spirit direct your thoughts and your words. For instance, today I would fill in the first line like this: BE confident that I am at work on your behalf.

BE_____

_____.

BE STRONG_____

_____.

BE STRONG AND_____

_____.

BE STRONG AND COURAGEOUS_____

_____.

BE STRONG AND COURAGEOUS FOR_____

_____.

BE STRONG AND COURAGEOUS FOR I_____

_____.

BE STRONG AND COURAGEOUS FOR I HAVE_____

_____.

BE STRONG AND COURAGEOUS FOR I HAVE GIVEN_____

_____.

BE STRONG AND COURAGEOUS FOR I HAVE GIVEN YOU_____

_____.

BE STRONG AND COURAGEOUS FOR I HAVE GIVEN YOU
THE_____.
BE STRONG AND COURAGEOUS FOR I HAVE GIVEN YOU THE
LAND_____.

CELEBRATING YOUR PROGRESS AND MOVING FORWARD

Climbing out of your comfort zone and soaring with God can unleash a host of emotions. Don't be surprised if at this point you feel excited, nervous, overwhelmed, and in awe of the vision given to you by Father God. He created you to be an amazing person and do amazing things. Perhaps you can relate to Mary when she asked the angel Gabriel, *"How can this be?"* (Luke 1:34). I have good news for you. It is God's job to bring your calling to pass. When you, like Mary who birthed our Savior, say to Holy Spirit, *"May it be done to me according to your word"* (Luke 1:38), you make way for the Lord to birth and mature the *so much more* that He has for you.

Perhaps you are like me when I have gotten hold of a vision and plan from the Lord. Once I have something written in my hand, I feel ready to jump right in and do the work that I see needs to be done to accomplish my cloud formation and my personal flight plan. God's timing, however, is critical to the success of any of life's journeys. It is worth the time and effort to wait until He reveals and confirms His timetable for your journey.

Before we go there, however, let's seal what the Lord has revealed in your Cloud Forming. Will you hold your Cloud Forming exercises in your hands as you pray with me?

> Lord, You are the Author of big audacious dreams and You are the Finisher of all of our plans. Father, in the name of Jesus, we give you the hopes and dreams, as well as the vision and plans that You have revealed to us on these pages. You alone know how the finished picture looks. We trust that You will lead us on the path to accomplish all that You ask of us. We let go of any preconceived notions and surrender our plans to You and Your will. Amen and Amen.

8.
Created For So Much More
UNDERSTANDING:
Determining
Your Timetable

Way to go! You have captured more of the vision that the Lord has for you and your life's purpose. You have soared into the sky and created cloud formations that are uniquely yours. I can practically hear you thinking, "That's nice, but what difference does that make for me today, tomorrow, next week, or next year?" Understanding God's timing is an important part of our journey of discovery, and that is what we are going to dig into next.

I call it God's timetable. Just as He has a vision and purpose for your life, He has a schedule set up just for you. The beauty of soaring with God is that He knows exactly the right steps to get you from here to there. He leads not only the direction of the step but also the length of the stride and the pace of the gait. Following His wisdom and guidance for your timing is powerful. It relieves the anxiety that comes when you ask, "When, Lord?"

It is easy to become overwhelmed when you look at cloud formations that seem too big to be true, require more risks than you're comfortable with, or reveal that many skills need honing. If we focus on the giant leap from here to there or keep our eyes too focused on the horizon, we can become discouraged and distracted. Combat these overwhelming feelings by seeing the flip side of dreaming big—working small.

As big as your dreams and visions may be, today is today and you are where you are in your journey. Your circumstances may not look like your future is attainable. You may not be able to see how you will ever get from here to there. Dear One, that is the Lord's job! He created you for your purpose and He is faithful to bring it to pass (1 Thessalonians 5:24). Give Him the responsibility to get you to the horizon. Today, look at the step that is in front of you and take that step. Dream big—yes—but work small. The adage about eating an elephant applies here. The answer to the question, "How do you eat an elephant?" is, "One bite at a time."

Dream with God. The Creator of the Universe has big plans for you as a world-changer. That doesn't mean that you will have a big platform or touch millions of lives. It does mean that you have the potential and, in fact, the responsibility to be the best in the world that surrounds you, whether your world is family, friends, colleagues, school, or church contacts. It also means that God wants you to influence and affect the world you live in for His Kingdom purposes. Perhaps your vision does show you on a big platform, but that platform seems far away, in reality.

Are you one who is looking at your dream, vision, and mission, and asking, "Why don't I see this coming to fruition in my life?" Big dreams can cause great frustration if you place your contentment there. My good friend Teasi Cannon (www.teasicannon.com), author of *My Big Bottom Blessing*,[17] is a wonderful speaker and teacher dedicated to sharing God's unconditional love. When we were eating lunch one day, she shared an interesting analogy that has stuck with me. She said that if we are constantly looking for the red carpet to be rolled out for us, we can miss the beautiful Oriental rug that is currently beneath our feet. Seeing the beauty at our feet here and now is a powerful picture of living in the moment.

I call this action of noticing what is in front of you "embracing the sacred now." Today becomes sacred when I rest in whatever the Lord is doing in my life this day. I am an artist. As an artist and visionary, it is easy for me to dream big. I can even work small. However, I admit that I can get impatient waiting for those big dreams to unfold. Live now. Embrace the present. There are people who need you today—right where you are. Do not get so focused on the future that you miss opportunity and divine appointments right now. Learn to be content, wherever you are, and ask the Lord about the step for the day.

I admit I have been challenged by this idea about taking small steps and waiting on the Lord as I have watched others have the success I thought I deserved. I have often thought of Paul's words:

> *For I have learned to be content in whatever circumstances I am* (Philippians 4:11).

Being content in whatever circumstance is a key to living in the sacred now. It is what makes it sacred. Paul wrote these words to his protégé Timothy:

But godliness actually *is a means of great gain when accompanied by contentment* (1 Timothy 6:6).

Godliness and contentment go hand in hand. Serving the Lord in a state of frustration and despair only brings further frustration and despair. Serving the Lord, while being content and living in the sacred now, brings great gain, including greater satisfaction with each step.

Don't rush ahead of God. Watch and listen for God's timetable. There will be times when He asks you to wait. There is purpose in the waiting. God has an appointed time for your big dream. The words from Habakkuk are encouraging and offer God's promise that He is at work—even if you don't see things moving forward.

"For the vision is yet for the appointed time; it hastens toward the goal and it will not fail. Though it tarries, wait for it; for it will certainly come, it will not delay" (Habakkuk 2:3).

While you allow God's timing to unfold in your life, diligently pursue Him. Seek Him about your current season, even if that means to rest when He says rest. God operates in cycles and seasons. When we come to better understand God's cyclical timing, we learn to be more content and are more able to joyfully live in the sacred now.

Simon and the Great Catch of Fish

The fifth chapter of Luke holds a glimpse into God's timing and the seasons of life. It is a story of a particular fishing trip.

Now it happened that while the crowd was pressing around Him and listening to the word of God, He was standing by the lake of Gennesaret; and He saw two boats lying at the edge of the lake; but the fishermen had gotten out of them and were washing their nets. And He got into one of the boats, which was Simon's, and asked him to put out a little way from the land. And he sat down and began teaching the people from the boat. When He had finished speaking, He said to Simon, "Put out into the deep water and let down your nets for a catch." Simon answered and said, "Master, we worked hard all night and caught nothing, but I will do as You say and let down the nets." When they had done this, they enclosed a great quantity of fish, and their nets began to break; so they signaled to their partners in the other boat for them to come and help them. And they came and filled both of the boats, so that they began to sink. But when

Simon Peter saw that, he fell down at Jesus' feet, saying, and "Go away from me Lord, for I am a sinful man!" For amazement had seized him and all his companions because of the catch of fish which they had taken (Luke 5:1–9).

Our story opens with Jesus. People were drawn to Him by His teaching. I find that comforting. It tells me that I don't have to implement a huge marketing strategy to carry out the ministry I am called to do. If I stay true to teaching the Word of God as He gives it, He will draw the audience. You may not be in ministry, but the truth is the same regardless of the nature of your call. Stay true to what the Lord has given you; He will bring those who need to hear your life message. In fact, God has ways to bring more than you could ever imagine.

In Jesus' case, the multitude was getting too big for Jesus to teach effectively. Take note of how He solves the problem. He doesn't ask where there is a bigger venue; He looks around and uses what is there: two empty boats. One becomes His speaking platform. Wherever you are, and whatever you are doing, God supplies you with what you need to accomplish your calling. He will always equip you if you keep your heart trained to see opportunity from Heaven's perspective. A fishing boat doesn't look like a speaking platform, but from Heaven's viewpoint, it is perfect. The boats are available to Jesus because the fishermen are done fishing and are cleaning their nets. I am not a fisherman, but my brother is. God orchestrated a fishing trip for me at just the right time.

When I was in Florida writing this book, my brother called to ask if I would like go out on their boat to fish. It was going to be a beautiful day out on the Gulf of Mexico. God said, "Rest," so I said "Yes."

How interesting that this fishing trip happened at the precise time when I was writing about Luke 5. During the course of our outing, my brother had to turn the boat back to shore because the waves grew higher and higher. The sea was too rough to risk going out any further.

No one caught any fish. Although I was there for a great boating day, the others in the boat were there to catch fish. Lesson 1: When fishermen go out to fish and catch nothing, it is a huge disappointment. At the end of the day, after the boat had been parked in its storage space, it took another hour at least to clean the boat, trailer, poles, and other equipment. Lesson 2: If fishing equipment is going to be used over and over, it must be cleaned every time it is used—whether or not fish have been caught.

God's timing is amazing. My own fishing experience brought greater insight to the process and emotions surrounding this passage in Luke 5. Let's look at it in the light of the lives of fisherman, and we will see what fishermen and non-fishermen alike can take away from this story.

Tending the Nets

As the story opens, the fishermen had left their boats and were washing their nets. One thing I can tell you from when I rode along with fishermen is that grass and other debris gets hooked by the fishing lines. Now imagine casting a net. The net is going to "catch" anything bigger than the holes in the net. Rocks, grass, and leaves are just a few things that could have ended up in the net. Even without catching fish, the nets need to be washed, cleaned, and mended of any tears. This process is tedious because every inch of the net must be examined, but the process is necessary for the nets to be useful the next time that they are needed.

Net-mending seasons in life bring time to do the work necessary to "clean and mend" our hearts, minds, and spirits. These times can feel frustrating until we reach a point of surrender to our Lord, rest in His timing, and ask what can be done to wash in His Word and/or seek the counsel of others. Perhaps this is the time to make an appointment for prayer or inner healing. Maybe it is time to take that webinar, read informative books, or take a retreat or sabbatical. Perhaps God says it's time to reconnect with family, friends, or colleagues. Think of this time as an opportunity to study, prepare, and ready yourself. Trust that God doesn't arbitrarily bring us into seasons of net cleaning.

A purpose and a plan exists for the net-cleaning or wilderness seasons of your life. During these times, you would probably rather be doing anything other than sitting and cleaning your nets. God is at work in those quiet moments, however. In recent years, I experienced a fairly long period when there was not much going on with ministry opportunities. When I told a friend that God had hit the pause button on my ministry, she disagreed profusely and showed me how much ministry I had done with family and friends. I had also used the time to work on several personal heart issues. I was indeed "doing the ministry"—it just looked different than I had expected. I was in a "cleaning my nets" season.

Do you find yourself in such a season? Be encouraged. The phone will ring with opportunity to do what you were created to do. The day will come when God says "Launch out."

Launch

Now that we've talked a bit about net-mending seasons of life, let's go back to our story in Luke 5. Jesus finishes preaching and ministering. He then turns to Simon and tells him to launch or put out into the deep water. Not only was this a directive to go fishing, but it was an instruction to launch out from shore. Notice Simon's reaction—it is one of dismay. This man has made a living fishing that lake. He knows the water, the best fishing spots, the best times to fish—and the best times not to fish. Think of him saying, "No way. I just spent the night fishing and didn't catch anything. I don't need any more frustration."

Fishermen can be a superstitious lot; they carry lucky hats and lucky fishing lures, and they have lucky fishing spots. The reverse is true as well; they easily become aware of anything that in their minds jinxes the catch. I, for instance, may never be invited on my brother's boat again because every time I'm there, no one catches any fish. I imagine Peter's emotions, like any fisherman after an unsuccessful expedition, are brimming with negativity after a nonproductive night, but he doesn't let his emotions stop him. What I love about Simon is his "nevertheless" attitude. In spite of feeling frustrated, disappointed, discouraged, and unlucky, he trusts Jesus. "Nevertheless." How many times have you faced those nevertheless moments?

- I don't want to forgive that offense; nevertheless....
- I don't feel comfortable making that phone call, writing that email, or having that meeting; nevertheless....
- I can't believe You are asking me to say this or do that; nevertheless....
- The doctors say cancer; nevertheless....

What happens when we, in spite of our misgivings, say "nevertheless" and follow Jesus' directions to *"launch out?"* Like Simon, we often find ourselves reaping such a huge harvest that it breaks our nets and we need help. In what appears to be a blink of an eye, Simon has shifted from cleaning his net to needing help with a monumental catch.

These shifts for Simon serve as a model of the times and seasons that the Lord uses to release us in our purpose, our destiny, and what we were created to do. God's timetable moves us from staying-put seasons of cleaning nets, to receiving His directive to launch, to reaping a harvest, to seeking help with abundant results. The times and seasons represented by this fishing story parallel how God works in our lives to bring about the vision that He has created. It also brings greater understanding of our role as we recognize the season we are in. Let's take a closer look at several ideas to help you along the journey of discovering the *so much more* that God has for you.

Cycles of God

Like the seasons of the year, God's timing is cyclical. The seasons of God come full circle: net-cleaning, launching, reaping a harvest, requiring help, net-cleaning, launching, reaping a harvest, requiring help, net-cleaning, and so on. It is in the quiet season of net-cleaning when you can clearly hear the Lord tell you to launch. When you launch in His timing, you will reap a great harvest. It may be so great that you require help. Ask for it. By asking someone to help when the "catch" is more than a single person can handle, you may be fulfilling someone else's destiny. And the cycle continues as you find yourself in another season of net-cleaning. This change in activity is not punishment. The comparative calm of net-cleaning may help prevent burn-out. As exciting as it may be, you are not created to be operating at your maximum speed or strength in every season of your life. Wherever you find yourself in this cycle, celebrate the season that God has you in now.

You are on your own path and in your own season. Where your neighbors, colleagues, sisters, or brothers are in their cycle is often completely different from where you are. Do not be jealous if they are in a full-net season and you are on the shore cleaning your net. Don't be prideful if you are launching and they are not. Understand you can both be in the perfect will of the Lord and be in completely different seasons of productivity at the same time. Like your unique timetable, your launch and harvest may look and feel completely different from another's.

Let's now take a look at various kinds of launches. When a boat leaves a dock, it is "launched." However, most marinas enforce no-wake zones for a good distance from shore. No-wake zones require minimum speeds for safety reasons. Even after you have launched into what the Lord has for you, it can take some time to get up to full speed. God has your well-being in mind. Be expectant without developing expectations about how quickly the Lord will move you forward in your journey. Consider this time of moving forward at a slow speed as on-the-job training while the Lord hones your skills, builds your foundations, and moves you forward in His timing.

The key to understanding and operating in God's itinerary is listening for His timing. When He says not now, it is not punishment—nor does it mean idleness. Waiting on the Lord is an active pursuit of Him and His plan and purpose for your life.

> *Yet those who wait for the LORD will gain new strength; they will mount up with wings like eagles, they will run and not get tired, they will walk and not become weary* (Isaiah 40:31).

The Hebrew word for wait in this verse is "qûvâh." According to Strong's Concordance, it means "to bind together (perhaps by twisting); to collect, expect; gather together, look, tarry, wait."[18] It isn't a passive, sit-on-your-hands, wait-for-someone-else-to-do-something kind of word. It is an active verb. Actively waiting on the Lord means taking the time you are given to study, learn, heal, and train. Consider a time of waiting to be a time of preparation for both the heart and your skill/talent. Then when God calls you to launch, you will be ready to run and not get tired, and you will be prepared to walk and not become weary. By staying connected to Holy Spirit in whatever season you find yourself, you will understand and align with His timetable as He speaks. I love this passage in Isaiah:

> *"Behold, the former things have come to pass, now I declare new things; before they spring forth I proclaim them to you"* (Isaiah 42:9).

Did you catch that? God's promise is that BEFORE new things spring forth, the Lord will proclaim them to you! He will prepare you. He will let you know when it is time to launch. That's His job—and His promise. God the Father, Son, and Holy Spirit walk with you daily. They will speak and lead you into all that They have created you to do. They will direct your steps on the path that releases you into the *so **much more*** that the Lord has for you to do. Wherever you are in this cycle of release, trust the Lord's hand and His itinerary. Lean in to Him. Sit at His feet while you wash, clean, and mend your net. Calm your spirit and listen.

There is purpose in the seasons of quiet and net-mending. Counterintuitive to our culture of immediate gratification and overly busy schedules, God tells us to sit awhile. Isaiah put it this way:

> *For thus the Lord God, the Holy One of Israel, has said,*
> *"In repentance and rest you will be saved.*
> *In quietness and trust is your strength"* (Isaiah 30:15).

If the Lord is asking you to be quiet as you mend your nets, He promises to strengthen you in the process. I assure you that if you give Him the time and space to speak, you will hear "Launch out." This promise comes later in Isaiah 30:

> *Although the LORD has given you bread of privation and water of oppression, He your Teacher will no longer hide Himself, but your eyes will behold your Teacher. Your ears will hear a word behind you, "This is the way, walk in it," whenever you turn to the right or to the left* (Isaiah 30:20–21).

This Scripture is one that is often misquoted. We tend to leave out the first part. The New King James Version of this verse uses the phrases *"bread of adversity and the water of affliction"* (Isaiah 30:20, NKJV). The Hebrew word for adversity is "tsar." It comes from a root word that means "narrow" or "tight place."[19] Sometimes the Lord puts us into tight places. The word affliction could be translated "to press."[20] The picture that emerges is of a tight place with little room to move while being pressed from all sides. God's promise is that He won't leave you in that tightly-pressed place. He will be heard as you surrender to His timing.

Strength to surrender to the Lord's timing comes during the time of quietness and rest. His promise is that He will no longer be hidden. You will hear Him when He says, *"Launch."* This promise is powerful! God assures us that we WILL see Him and hear Him, our Teacher. Seasons pass. It has been said that if you are not currently in a stormy season, you are moving into or coming out of one.

Remember that no season lasts forever as you live contentedly in whatever season you find yourself. Enjoy those seasons when the Lord says *"Launch"* and everything looks fresh and new because you are finally leaving the shore. **They too will pass.**

Treasure the seasons when the harvest begins to come in. **They too will pass.**

Rejoice in the seasons when your harvest is more than you can handle and the favor and goodness of the Lord is abundantly clear in your life. **They too will pass.**

Honor and thank the Lord for the seasons of mending your net. Sometimes they can bring the most intimate times with Him. They are seasons of strengthening and preparing for what lies ahead. And **they too will pass.**

Responding to God in All Seasons

We cannot leave this story without recognizing how the night of fishing ends. What is Simon's reaction to the great catch of fish? Let's take a look.

> *But when Simon Peter saw that, he fell down at Jesus' feet, saying, "Go away from me Lord, for I am a sinful man, O Lord!" For amazement had seized him and all his companions because of the catch of fish which they had taken* (Luke 5:8–9).

Peter's falling at Jesus' feet shows a reverence to His Lord. His statement of repentance here seems to come from a heart of worship and recognition that Jesus, not Peter, was and is the one in control. Worship opens hearts and minds to the goodness of God, His provision, and His perfect timing in our lives. Certainly, we should worship the Lord through all seasons of our lives, whether net-mending or pulling in a great catch. Staying in the Presence of God through worship is what keeps our hearts, minds, and spirits tuned in to God's timetable. Before we move on to our exercise, I want to share a couple additional nuggets that can be gleaned from this story.

First, let's consider what happened when Simon and the others went out in their own timing. They had been out all night and had not caught anything. This incident reminds us that we can be in God's perfect timing and still not see results in the natural. Take heart in the fact that God had you launch for a reason, even if you can't see it. **God's seasons have purpose and are perfectly-timed even if you don't experience the results you hoped for.**

Our second nugget reminds us that we can thwart God's perfectly-timed cycle when we decide to take matters into our own hands. The futility of empty nets after fishing all night shows us what can happen when we decide to "launch" before we have heard instructions and confirmations from the Lord. Running when you are to be walking, and acting prematurely or launching in your own strength dooms you to empty and torn nets that require even more time to clean and mend. Wait for the Lord's timing. It is critical not only to know the "what" of God's call but also the "when."

Understanding the times and season that you are in is extremely valuable. If God has you in a season of mending nets, and you are trying to launch, you will find yourself frustrated. If you are in a season of harvest, and you take too much time to rest, you will miss the harvest that He has for you. Recognizing the season of God that you are in has significant impact on reaching your desired destination. Because of this importance, take a few minutes to connect Simon's story to your own.

SOARING WITH GOD

Exercise 19: Seasons and Cycles

Now it's time to sit with the Lord once again. Grab your notebook, ask yourself these questions, and write your reflections.

1. Am I mending my nets? Is the Lord asking me to sit quietly and work on heart or character issues? When was the last time I was in that season? What did the Lord teach me?
2. Do I find myself launching out from the shore in God's timing? Have opportunities arisen that require me to take a leap of faith into the deep waters of my calling? What speed am I traveling? Is God doing some on-the-job training as I travel in a no-wake zone, or am I going full-throttle toward my destination?
3. Am I reaping a harvest? Do I see results or am I hearing testimonies that what I am doing is bearing fruit in others' lives or contributing to an organization's success? Has the Lord shown me the Kingdom impact that I am having?
4. Do I need help because the harvest is more than I can handle? Am I a little overwhelmed by all that the Lord is doing on my behalf, and am I having a hard time getting my part done? Is there someone I can ask for assistance? Who is it? What can they do for me?
5. Do I feel frustrated because I launched outside of God's timetable? Do I feel like I am beating my head against the wall? Am I weary of working with no results?
6. Through it all, have I taken time to worship the Lord in my current season? Use this time to give thanks verbally or in writing and worship the Lord of the Harvest.

It can be gut-wrenching to ask yourself these questions. Perhaps you have realized that you are not in the season that you thought or hoped you might be by now. I know it can be disappointing, but it's also helpful, because recognition of your cycle with God is a great starting place to propel you forward.

The next step is to ask yourself:

1. What am I doing to assist the Lord, or to co-labor with Him in my assignment?
2. How can I multiply what the Lord is doing in my life?

Knowing where you are in God's timetable is foundational to understanding what He is asking you to do today. Equipped with an understanding of your specific time and season with God, you can make wise and productive decisions about the work that is and is NOT at hand. For example, spending time planning a ministry fundraising event when the Lord has asked you to mend relationships is not operating within the timing of God. It would be wiser and more productive to spend relational time when mending is needed. Then schedule and plan the fundraiser when God says, "Launch." Each day brings choices to be made to co-labor with God. Aligning your choices with your season will propel you forward in your flight path toward the destiny of who God created you to be and what He created you to do.

Use God's timetable to help make your daily choices. When I ask those I coach, "What are you doing today or tomorrow to reach your vision?" I often hear a list of unrelated tasks that have no cohesion or common goal. These answers might be expected since I largely work with creative people, entrepreneurs, and start-up ministries. Typically, these groups have big visions and seem to have no difficulty dreaming with God. Their cloud formations are large and often encompass several sheets of paper. Examining God's itinerary serves as a plumb line to begin to sort out the necessary, unrelated, and the "now or not now" actions that might spring up from their cloud formations. They start to evaluate how to separate the tasks that are for future projects from those that are to be done today.

When you ask God what to do today, apply the key strategies of working small, living now, and taking the next step in front of you as you leave the destination to the Lord. Each day is a new opportunity to advance your dream, vision, and Kingdom purposes right where you are. As you co-labor with God to accomplish the vision that He has planted within you, steps can always be taken today, tomorrow, and this week. Listen to the guidance of Holy Spirit. In the same way that we saw Simon Peter advancing through God's cycles, Holy Spirit will guide and advance you through His itinerary.

I am certain that at this very moment you have any number of ideas floating around in your head that are connected to your destiny. Now is the time to list, sort, and prioritize those ideas into action items.

Exercise 20: Ten Steps

The next exercise is a consistent favorite among conference attendees. Take the necessary time to complete it. Don't rush through it. Once again, grab your notebook or journal and turn to a fresh page. Number it one to 10 along the left side.

Go back to the list you created in Exercise 17 in the previous chapter. Ask the Lord to highlight 10 steps from that list that you can take right here in your sacred now. If you haven't written 10 yet, ask the Lord to give you the remainder of the steps now. Do you need to write those emails? Is it time to register and attend that webinar that would give you the information you need to move forward? Do you need to make that phone call to set up a meeting with a contact the Lord has highlighted? Is it time to volunteer with that ministry, church, or school? Perhaps you need to purchase painting supplies or a new computer. God is not asking for perfection here, but He does ask for faithfulness and obedience. **Write a list of at least 10 things that will help you realize your destiny, with no order of importance.**

Man's Plans, God's Steps

Great job! I pray that you are getting a sense of the steps that the Lord has put before you. As with all of the exercises in this book, repeat this one periodically. Conference and workshop attendees often tell me the very exercises you are doing continue to bring revelation and value as they redo them. That's because there is never just one list, one cloud formation, one step to take as you move through God's cycle of release. There is one step to take today. One step that is in God's order for you. Planning is well and good, but allow Holy Spirit to direct your next step.

The mind of man plans his way, but the Lord directs his steps (Proverbs 16:9).

Within your heart, you can make plans for your future,
But the Lord chooses the steps you take to get there (Proverbs 16:9,
The Passion Translation, TPT).

A man's mind plans his way, but the Lord directs his steps and *makes them sure* (Proverbs 16:9, Amplified Bible, Classic Edition, AMPC).

Notice that none of these translations of this popular verse implies that we are not to make our plans. What is clear is that **as we make plans, we must seek the Lord to ensure the right step is taken at the right time.** Consulting the Lord before taking a step or doing a task is imperative. As counterintuitive as it may seem, the God of the Universe cares about the appointments you make, the emails you write, or the classes you take.

Perhaps the idea of asking our big, audacious God for itty-bitty steps seems too practical for you. Are you more accustomed to including the Lord in your spiritual life, but not comfortable asking Him for directions, instructions, wisdom, and guidance on your day-to-day tasks and projects? Allow me to share a couple of personal examples of God's interest and desire to become a part of your daily destiny journey.

I am a professional visual artist/painter because the Lord took me by the hand and showed me how to paint. Several years ago, after more than 20 years as a fiber artist, I wanted to learn to paint. There I sat, canvas before me, as I asked Holy Spirit to lead me. My prayer was simple. "Holy Spirit, I don't know how to do this, but you do. Would you please teach me?" And He did.

Lest you think I was overstepping some doctrine that says I was using God for my own purposes and gain, consider what Jesus told the disciples.

"But the Helper, the Holy Spirit, whom the Father will send in My name, He will teach you all things, and bring to your remembrance all that I said to you" (John 14:26).

That's a red-letter verse! That is Jesus teaching the disciples about the Holy Spirit. What is the Greek meaning of the word "all"? According to Strong's Concordance it is: "all, any, every, the whole."[21] In other words, all means all! For me, that included painting. The Apostle John heard Jesus teach the "all" of the Holy Spirit.

John penned another verse that highlights this same practical nature of Holy Spirit.

As for you, the anointing which you received from Him abides in you, and you have no need for anyone to teach you but as His anointing teaches you about all things, and is true and is not a lie, and just as it has taught you, you abide in Him (1 John 2:27).

Anointing here refers to a special endowment of the Holy Spirit. Put another way, your anointing is your unique mix of gifts, talents, and calling. It is that which abides in you. It includes those special attributes that make you uniquely qualified to be what you were created to be and to do what you were created to do. The Holy Spirit abides in you. He is the fullness—the completion—the master of any anointing. In the same way that a master painter teaches an apprentice or student, His Presence can and will teach you *"about all things."* Once again, the Greek word "all" means, "all, any, every, the whole." All means all. Even the most practical and seemingly unspiritual things in life are available to us through the power of the Holy Spirit. Even technology is not beyond God's scope.

Some time ago, I needed a set of digital slides for a webinar that I was going to be leading. In previous years, every time I had gone to use the software such as Power Point for slide presentations, I could not figure it out. I am reasonably savvy about technology, but when it came to that particular program, it was like Greek to me. When I opened the program, I felt as if I were reading another language. In the past, my husband and I had worked out a method by which I would let him know what I needed on each slide and he would put the presentation together. This time, however, his plate was full, and I knew I couldn't burden him with another project.

There I sat with my computer before me, and I sought the Lord with a similar prayer that I had prayed about painting years earlier. "Holy Spirit, I do not understand this program, but Your Word tells me that You will teach me all things, and I need to understand this program." After sitting quietly with the Lord, I opened the slide presentation program. It was if something just connected in my brain. What before had looked like indecipherable hieroglyphics, suddenly made enough sense to me that I could navigate through and finish the presentation that I needed. It truly was miraculous! Miracles happen when you invite Holy Spirit to work with and in you.

God loves to work alongside His children. He delights to help us change the world—one painting or one computer program at a time. Leaning in to Him for help should become a way of life. Anytime you feel yourself thinking, "I won't bother the God of the Universe for this," imagine that you are the parent of a child who needs what you know to succeed. Now imagine that child not asking for help. It would hurt you, wouldn't it? How much more does your Heavenly Father long to assist you in accomplishing the very thing that He created you for? He is waiting to help you take the step that is before you. That is the point of the next exercise.

Exercise 21: The Next Steps

Allowing God to order your footsteps means giving Him time and space to prioritize the tasks and steps before you. Of the 10 steps or action items that you listed in the last exercise, God knows the order and priority of each. Conference attendees tell me this exercise is one of the most helpful and productive because it brings immediate results when put into action. Don't skip it!

Take a look at your list of 10 items. Ask the Lord to highlight three of them. Which three is He saying "now" to? **Star or highlight those three steps.**

Next, take a look at those three steps and a look at your calendar. Next to each of the three steps, write the date by which you will accomplish that step. Be realistic but also challenge yourself. Giving yourself a deadline is a powerful way of setting goals that get done. Deadlines may feel confining to you, but do not let that stop you.

The Importance of Deadlines

Deadlines are like boundaries. They keep us on task and in step with God's order to accomplish our vision. Like a river that floods its banks and flows without direction, we can go astray from our vision and purpose without the boundaries that deadlines provide. Setting a date for yourself to accomplish your step/goals keeps you on task. Deadlines keep you operating in your vision and on your mission.

You need a vision for your life to know where your flight plan is taking you, but vision without a plan and timetable is only one side of the equation for doing what you were created to do. King Solomon in his book of Proverbs gives this insight:

> *"Where there is no vision, the people are unrestrained, But happy is he who keeps the law"* (Proverbs 29:18).

> *When there is no clear prophetic vision*
> *People wander astray.*
> *But when you follow the revelation of the Word*

Heaven's bliss fills your soul! (Proverbs 29:18, The Passion Translation, TPT).

Allow me to paraphrase the truth of this proverb in light of listing steps and adding deadlines. The Deborah Gall translation is: "Without clear vision, you wander day-to-day doing this and that. With a clear vision and a step-by-step path, you will live joyfully knowing you are operating as who you were created to be, doing what you were created to do."

CELEBRATING YOUR PROGRESS AND MOVING FORWARD

Way to Go! You have stretched yourself and cast your net according to God's timing. As you soar with Holy Spirit and allow Him to order your footsteps, you acquire the *so much more* understanding of who He is and how He operates. As you align your daily steps with His timetable, you are on the most direct flight path to reach your destination of being all that He created you to be and accomplishing all that He created you to do. God's flight plan—even though it may include layovers and rest stops—is still the most direct way to reach your destination. It is important to gain wisdom about the times in your journey when it feels like God slows you down almost to a halt. Just as knowing God's cycles and seasons brings greater understanding, learning to soar and rest at the same time brings enjoyment during God's layovers. Understanding and learning how to handle those layover times is the next stop in our journey.

Once again, before we go any further, let's take a moment to pray.

Holy Spirit, I ask that You bring greater insight and understanding for each person reading this chapter and this prayer. Will You reveal Your plan, Your timetable, and Your season for each life represented? Fill Your children with Your grace—Your empowering Presence—which enables them to be who You created them to be and do what You created them to do—in Your timing. In the name that is above all names, Jesus the Christ, Amen.

9.
Created For So Much More
REST:
Enjoying the Layovers

Layovers are often a part of traveling. Sometimes people spend more time sitting in an airport than actually being on an airplane. Soaring with God—living out who you were created to be and what you were created to do—can feel like a layover at times. You may find yourself antsy to move forward, but it feels as if the Lord has hit the pause button. You may be full of vision and purpose, yet you find yourself bogged down with the mundane tasks of life. Or perhaps life just feels dry—with no inspiration, revelation, or vision whatsoever. These times are often called wilderness seasons. God has purpose in even the driest of seasons. Let's take a look at a few examples and strategies that will help you gain more rest and enjoyment when the Lord takes you into a wilderness season.

No journey in life is complete without the visits to places that feel more like the dry and weary land of a desert or wilderness than the lush, bountiful, ripe-for-harvest landscape of a "Promised Land." In *The Book of Mysteries*, Jonathan Cahn gives this insight to the wilderness: "In Hebrew, the wilderness is called the *midbar*. *Midbar* comes from the root word *davar*. And *davar* means to speak. What is the wilderness? It is the *midbar*. And what is the midbar? It is the place of God's speaking, the place of His voice."[22] One purpose of wilderness seasons is that they give a time and place without distraction to listen and hear what the Lord is saying. These seasons also provide a time and place for re-evaluation.

While flying from one place to another, layovers offer an opportunity to double-check travel itineraries and reservations. The same can be true in the journey of destiny. Layovers of life offer a good time to do a little analysis. One of the reasons God hits "pause" is to provide us time to catch up before we move forward. This pause could be the perfect time to make that appointment to address heart issues. Perhaps it is time to shore up the foundation of the ministry or business by rewriting your vision or mission statement. Ask yourself, "Are my skills sufficient to handle the increase that the Lord has for me?" No matter what your answer is, take advantage of the layovers. They offer you the opportunity to be more prepared for the next season of release, which is the time when the Lord has you operating in what you were created to do in a greater capacity.

Hone Your Skills

Whether you call it a wilderness or a layover, the time when your schedule is not full of doing your destiny is a great time to hone your skills. Room for improvement always exists. Use this time to compare the vision in your spirit with your present-day capabilities. See any discrepancies? Often times, in my layovers, I realize that I need a higher level of skill to accomplish what I see myself doing in the future.

One example of these times was when Holy Spirit led me step-by-step to participate in a webinar for the purpose of improving my skills in public speaking. This webinar rocked my world, and I knew the Lord was showing me something significant for my future. As I watched the improvement others made as they were coached in public speaking, I heard God's whisper to take note. He had something to show me. I knew that I had work to do. I was a good teacher/speaker, but the Lord showed me the *so much more* that He had for me. He showed me that I could be so much better. When I went to bed that night, I came face to face with the disparity between my current skill level and the vision I had. This kind of disparity in skill may be witnessed at musical concerts.

Think about going to a concert by your favorite musical performer. The opening act comes on stage and is really good. It requires a better-than-average musician to open for a popular headliner. These people are certainly gifted. The next band comes out and they are even better. Yet, when the headliner begins to play, you immediately understand why that artist has top billing. Headliners have honed their skills, my friends. You could be a headliner. Do not waste the layovers in your destiny journey. Listen to the Lord for anything He may want to say. Spend the layovers working on your heart, restructuring your work, and/or honing your skills. Listen to the Lord for any way that He may want to transform your layover into productive preparation time.

Keep Walking

Even when the circumstances in your life do not match the vision you carry of your destiny and future, do not stall. Work is to be done during the layovers of life. Keep putting one foot in front of the other in whatever the Lord is showing you and calling you to do.

Layovers can feel like fog where you cannot see where you are heading. Like driving through fog, it may be time to slow down, to listen, and to seek the Lord for how and when to take the next step. It is human nature to see fog as something that hinders forward progress and hampers the journey of life. I would suggest, however, that a change of perspective is in order. Fog is actually clouds touching the Earth; it could be considered Heaven touching Earth. God led the Israelites through the wilderness as a pillar of cloud by day (Exodus 13:21). The cloud of God was the fog that led them. It was also His manifest Presence in the Tabernacle.

Then the cloud covered the tent of meeting, and the glory of the LORD *filled the tabernacle* (Exodus 40:34).

The concept here is God's "shekinah" glory, meaning His Presence manifested in cloud form. The word "shekinah" can be translated as "dwelling" or "Presence of God."[23] When you feel you are in a fog, perhaps you are more in the Presence of God than ever. As you dwell in that fog, that cloud of God's Presence, allow Him to speak. Sitting with God is never standing still. It is always a means of moving forward.

Grab hold of the hand of the One who walks with you and keep walking. It may be time to take baby steps, but steps are always there to be taken. We all have times when our vision is clouded as if we are walking in a fog. Heaven moves on your behalf, even when you feel as though you are standing still. Your forward movement may not be obvious to you or to the world, but trust God's purpose. God uses the layovers and hidden seasons of our lives to continue to work in, through, and for us. Rather than being frustrated by these times, know that you are in good company. Jesus Himself lived most of His life hidden from public view.

Biblical Examples

By the age of 12, Jesus knew His destiny and purpose. He knew who He was created to be and what He was created to do. We know this because of His response to His parents when they found Him in the synagogue.

"Why is it that you were looking for Me? Did you not know that I had to be in My Father's house?" (Luke 2:49).

Many translations replace *"in My Father's house"* with *"be about My Father's business."* That is purpose and destiny language. It implies that Jesus knew the work that He was called to do on Earth. Yet there is little written about the next 18 years of His life. Being fully man, he must have awakened every morning wondering if this was the day when He would begin to finally walk out what He was put on Earth to accomplish.

A look at the bigger picture reveals that Jesus lived a "hidden" life for 30 years. We know much more about His final three years when He was in public ministry than we know of His first 30. Therefore, 90 percent of His life was in the hidden place. Only 10 percent of His life here on Earth was in public ministry. Jesus was not the only biblical character who experienced the "hidden season" of God—that place of wilderness and layover. Moses, Abraham, Elijah, David, and others understood what it was like to live a life of destiny and hiddenness at the same time.

Let's take a closer look at David's experience to see what the Lord does in the hidden seasons of life. David is first mentioned in 1 Samuel 16 after God had told Samuel to go to the house of Jesse to anoint the next king. Saul was still on the throne at this time so there was no apparent need for an heir to the throne. Samuel obeyed God's directive anyway and began to search for the next king to anoint.

> *And Samuel said to Jesse, "Are these all the children?" And he said, "There remains yet the youngest, and behold, he is tending sheep. Then Samuel said to Jesse, "Send and bring him; for we will not sit down until he comes here"* (1 Samuel 16:11).

David was the youngest of the family. His own father did not consider David as a candidate for king. In addition to his birth order, David was a shepherd. Shepherds were not highly esteemed in terms of profession. So to summarize, when we first meet David, he is low on the family end of importance.

> *Then Samuel took the horn of oil and anointed him in the midst of his brothers; and the Spirit of the LORD came mightily upon David from that day forward* (1 Samuel 16:13).

Samuel anointed David to be king of Israel. Now that was a big dream, vision, and mission! But this anointing was more than a prophetic word, it was a prophetic act straight from Heaven as evidenced by the Spirit of the Lord coming upon David mightily.

What happens next is important for us to understand. Is David ushered into the presence of Saul to begin his training? Not at all. All that can be deduced from the remaining text in 1 Samuel is that David is sent back to continue tending the sheep. He has been anointed king and finds himself alone on the hills with a bunch of sheep! How's that for a layover and hidden season?

Lesson from the Wilderness

The layovers of life are full of lessons to be learned. David learned that he could trust the Lord to deliver him in times of need. Listen in as David speaks to Saul:

"Your servant has killed both the lion and the bear; and this uncircumcised Philistine will be like one of them, since he has taunted the armies of the living God." And David said, "The LORD who delivered me from the paw of the lion and from the paw of the bear, He will deliver me from the hand of this Philistine" (1 Samuel 17: 36–37).

David had experienced God's hand of deliverance in the wilderness. He knew God to be faithful and trustworthy. Why did God have him there? God was building something even greater than character in David in the wilderness—God was building an intimate relationship with David. The Lord gave David experiences to remember and rely on when FUTURE adversities arose. He does the same for you.

When you are in life's layovers, you experience God in ways that you cannot experience any other way. He takes you through hidden and wilderness seasons to show you who He is and who you are not. He builds relationship with you in those times because, as I have said before, He is more concerned with being in relationship with you than anything else.

Nothing is ever hidden from God's perspective even if it appears hidden to the world. If you find yourself in a layover, a wilderness season, or a hidden place, rest in God's goodness and grace to endure. This time is for seeking the Lord for greater understanding and revelation. Trust that He has a plan and a purpose for this season. Ask Him to show you what work He is doing in you. Train yourself to be content in every season and circumstance. It is a challenge, but well worth the effort.

Allowing the Lord to show you His perspective during this time in your life is a healthy exercise no matter where you are. You may not be in a hidden place or a wilderness season. Great! It is still a meaningful exercise to check in with the Lord regarding His timing. Continually seek Heaven's viewpoint for your life. The next exercise does just that.

SOARING WITH GOD

Exercise 22: Be Still

One of the lessons that the Lord teaches us in layover seasons is that He is God and we are not. This exercise reinforces that truth and brings peace, contentment, and revelation. Psalm 46:10 is an often-quoted: *"Be still and know that I am God."* The phrase "be still" can also be interpreted as relax, let go, or cease striving. All are powerful phrases to keep in mind as you consider what the Lord is doing in your life.

Use this exercise as a powerful tool to reveal more about the Lord, to help you see His hand at work in your life, and to gain His perspective, even in the hidden and wilderness seasons.

Use the prompts to fill in the rest of the sentence. Lean in to Holy Spirit and let Him fill in the blanks on your behalf.

BE_____

_____.

BE STILL_____

_____.

BE STILL AND_____

_____.

BE STILL AND KNOW_____

_____.

BE STILL AND KNOW THAT_____

_____.

BE STILL AND KNOW THAT I_____

_____.

BE STILL AND KNOW THAT I AM_____

_____.

BE STILL AND KNOW THAT I AM GOD_____

_____.

If I did this exercise today my first sentence would say BE patient, I have everything under control and all will be fulfilled in its correct timing. The last sentence might say, BE STILL AND KNOW THAT I AM GOD, I knew you before I formed you and ordained every day that you have lived. Trust Me in all things. Trust that I will bring your dreams to pass as you walk with Me daily.

As I reflect on the revelation that has poured from Heaven when people have done this exercise, I am led to pray:

> Lord, You alone are God. You are Creator and Redeemer. You created us for *so much more,* and You redeemed our life from the pit for Kingdom purpose. Holy Spirit, You whisper to our hearts and spirits and tell us Truth that will bring us into the fullness of who You created us to be and what You created us to do. Forgive us when we keep moving when You say, "Rest." Help us to be still and know in the depths of our beings that You alone are God. We give you our plans, our timetables, and our preconceived notions of how things are to work. We give you all honor and glory, forever! In Jesus' name, Amen.

CELEBRATING YOUR PROGRESS AND MOVING FORWARD

As you continue on your journey to realize the *so much more* of who you were created to be and what you were created to do, rely on the Lord to show you His plan and purpose for those seasons in your life that may feel dry, dull, and lonely. Be grateful that your flight path is known by the One who sits on the throne. Rather than fighting these times, learn to be content where you are and to keep walking and worshipping. By enjoying the layovers God has for your life, you will bring *so much more* rest to your spirit as you soar with God and allow Him to be the God of *so much more.* Dear One, I know He has *so much more* across the board for you! Even in the midst of the turbulence of life, God has great things for you to learn, unlock, and explore. The key is to know how God asks us to navigate through stormy times, which is where our journey takes us next.

10.
Created For So Much More
PEACE:
Navigating Through Storms

Seldom does one fly without hitting turbulence somewhere along the way. Delays and cancellations of flights because of inclement weather are an expected part of travel. Driving doesn't prevent additional delays either, with potential road twists and turns, detours, slow downs, and complete stops. The journey you travel toward your destiny is not any different. Things don't always flow smoothly—Jesus didn't promise that they would. Quite the opposite. Jesus clearly tells us that if we are operating on His behalf, we will face trials and tribulations (John 16:33). His prayer for His disciples and for us as future believers shows us just that.

"I have given them Your word; and the world has hated them, because they are not of the world, even as I am not of the world. I do not ask You to take them out of the world, but to keep them from the evil one. They are not of the world, even as I am not of the world. Sanctify them in the truth; Your word is truth. As you sent Me into the world, I also have sent them into the world" (John 17:14–18).

If you are operating within the fullness of your *so much more*—who you were created to be and what you were created to do—you will hit opposition. How do you overcome those obstacles and keep moving forward? You get equipped to navigate through the challenges in confidence and peace. Learning to handle the frustrations of the journey is critical to staying on your flight path. Implementing specific strategies will align you with Jesus the Overcomer and teach you to successfully endure the storms of life with His help and guidance. Let's take a look at the life of King David for a great example of living an overcoming life.

Strengthen Yourself in the Lord
David faced tremendous trials before he became king. Upon returning to

battle in Chapter 30 of 1 Samuel, David and his men find their wives and children gone and the city burned. Their families had been taken captive by the Amalekites. David wept with his people *"until there was no strength in them to weep"* (1 Samuel 30:4). That didn't satisfy the people as we see a few verses later.

> *Moreover David was greatly distressed because the people spoke of stoning him, for all the people were embittered, each one because of his sons and daughters. But David strengthened himself in the LORD his God* (1 Samuel 30:6).

We must learn to strengthen ourselves in the Lord our God as David did. In the New Testament, Paul gives the same message to the Ephesians,

> *Finally, be strong in the Lord, and in the strength of His might* (Ephesians 6:10).

We must learn to strengthen ourselves in the Lord because He is the One who has already procured the victory. Every obstacle we face is rooted in satan's desire to throw us off track. His purpose is to distract us from our God-given destiny and purpose and to cause us to doubt ourselves and ultimately to doubt God, our Creator and Savior. We must be aware of the enemy and his tactics if we are to stay strong in the Lord.

Jesus described the enemy in the Gospel of John.

> *"The thief comes only to steal and kill and destroy; I came that they may have life, and have it abundantly"* (John 10:10).

As much as I'd love to just focus on Jesus' overcoming power, we need to understand the enemy to recognize his schemes, so I'm going to spend a bit more time on him. It is my experience that satan can be as content to hurt, harm, and hinder as he is to steal, kill, and destroy. Make no mistake about it, satan is quite pleased with the complacency and slumber of the children of God. He will bring distraction and resistance when he senses children of the Almighty God waking up to their God-given purpose and destiny. He knows more than you do that he is a defeated foe and that victory is already yours through Christ. He works to keep you from living in that truth.

Paul reinforces this understanding of the forces that are against you when he writes to the Ephesians about putting on the armor of God.

For our struggle is not against flesh and blood, but against the rulers, against the powers, against the world forces of this darkness, against the spiritual *forces of wickedness in the heavenly* places (Ephesians 6:12).

Paul is telling the Ephesians to be aware of the spiritual enemy they fight. When he goes on to describe the armor of God and tells them to put it on, he is instructing them to be ready and equipped to defend themselves against the storms that the enemy would throw at them (Ephesians 6:13–17).

Prayer

Paul ends his instructions with a word of advice that is as valid for us today as it was for the Ephesians.

With all prayer and petitions pray at all times in the Spirit, and with this in view, be on the alert with all perseverance and petition for all the saints (Ephesians 6:18).

Prayer is one of the most important tools you have to overcome the forces that come against you as you walk out your purpose and advance the Kingdom of God. That seems almost too obvious doesn't it? You may be saying, "Of course, I pray! I ask God to remove this storm every day." Prayer is meant to be more than just asking God for help. Prayer is time spent communicating with God in such a way that it becomes part of a larger worship experience. In that greater context, prayer ushers in the Presence of God and reveals *so much more* of Him. Worship—of the One who created you and your purpose—is a significant tool to help you move through the storms of life.

Worship

A posture of worship acknowledges God for who He is. When you worship and honor Him, you take your hands off the issues of life and give Him control. Whatever your form of worship, profess who God is. Play music. Dance. Sing. Make declarations. Speak Scripture aloud. Read the Psalms. The list of worship ideas is as endless and unique as the children of God. Atmospheres change when you worship and acknowledge God Your Maker, Redeemer, and Comforter. Take a look at this beautiful image of worship in Isaiah.

Sing to the LORD *a new song,*
Sing His praise from the end of the earth!
You who go down to the sea, and all that is in it.
You islands, and those who dwell on them.
Let the wilderness and its cities lift up their voices,
The settlements where Kedar inhabits.
Let the inhabitants of Sela sing aloud,
Let them shout for joy from the tops of the mountains.
Let them give glory to the LORD
And Declare His praise in the coastlands (Isaiah 42:10–12).

The next verse is revelatory. It shows that God responds to worship that acknowledges Him and gives honor to what He has done. The act of worship moves God to action on your behalf! Hallelujah!

The Lord will go forth like a warrior,
He will arouse His zeal like a man of war.
He will utter a shout, yes, He will raise a war cry.
He will prevail against His enemies (Isaiah 42:13).

Your enemies are God's enemies and He will not be defeated. By praising and worshipping the Lord, you grant Him access, permission, and space to move and work on your behalf. He will let you do things in your own strength, but He'd rather not. He'd rather flex His muscles and defeat the enemies in your life.

The fact that God responds to our acts of worship shows us that He co-labors with us to overcome the challenges in our lives. What that means is that you have work to do if you are to overcome the enemy and navigate through the storms of life. You must take responsibility for your life and your choices. As I shared in Chapter 2, you can choose life, light, and blessing or you can choose death, darkness, and despair. Choosing wisely is not only important for your freedom, but for handling life's storms as well. Your mindset determines which end of the life and death spectrum you choose— that's why you must learn to control your thoughts.

Take Your Thoughts Captive

It takes awareness and discipline to choose life, light, and blessing when the lights seem low and things aren't going smoothly. It is difficult to be joyful when surrounded by grief and pain. I am not suggesting that you "fake it until you make it." There are times when sorrow, grief, and even pain are appropriate—God can handle those emotions and will give you the strength to do the same. It becomes destructive, however, when mourning turns to despair or grieving becomes self-pity. At those times, heed Paul's wise instructions to take your thoughts captive.

For though we walk in the flesh, we do not war according to the flesh, for the weapons of our warfare are not of the flesh, but divinely powerful for the destruction of fortresses. We are *destroying speculations and every lofty thing raised up against the knowledge of God, and* we are *taking every thought captive to the obedience of Christ* (2 Corinthians 10:3–5).

This process of taking your thoughts captive to the obedience of Christ can be tough, I know, but it is necessary for victory. All too often, I counsel those who seem to be quite content with their thoughts of doubt, distress, discouragement, and even despair. Those four "D" words spell Destruction with a capital D. Scripture is full of the truth of God that dispels and defeats those lies of the enemy. In fact, Scripture becomes a very handy and useful tool in taking thoughts captive when you replace the lies of the enemy with the truth of God's Word.

Jesus showed us just how to take our thoughts captive when He encountered the devil in the wilderness in Luke 4. For every temptation that the devil threw out, Jesus used scripture as a rebuttal:

Jesus answered him, "It is written, 'MAN SHALL NOT LIVE ON BREAD ALONE' " (Luke 4:4).

Jesus answered him, "It is written, 'YOU SHALL WORSHIP THE LORD YOUR GOD AND SERVE HIM ONLY' " (Luke 4:8).

Jesus answered and said to him, "It is said 'YOU SHALL NOT PUT THE LORD YOUR GOD TO THE TEST' " (Luke 4:12).

"It is written" or "God's Word says" is a great place to start in taking thoughts captive and replacing satan's lies with God's truth. Here are a few examples.

1. When the enemy says, "You can't do it," God's Word says, *"I can do all things through Christ who strengthens me"* (Philippians 4:13, NKJV).

2. When the father of lies says, "You will never amount to much," Your heavenly Father says, *You are worth enough that I sent my son to die for you* (paraphrase of John 3:16).

3. When fear comes to attack, Jesus says that His perfect love abiding in you casts out all fear (1 John 4:18).

4. When sorrow pulls you under, Holy Spirit brings peace that passes understanding (Philippians 4:7).

For every lie that the enemy would bring to your mind, there is truth written in the Bible. When you can't seem to find that truth, simply speak the name of Jesus. It was the person of Jesus who overcame the world. Christ is in you as your Hope and Source of peace and joy. He has defeated every weapon of the enemy. By speaking Jesus' name out loud, you call on Him as the Lord of Hosts and the Captain of the angel armies, and they move on your behalf. You join with that army of angels when you speak life over yourself.

Be Absorbed

Throughout this book, you have been prophesying life over yourself and your destiny. From the first exercise to the last, you have asked Holy Spirit to guide you and the Lord to speak His words of life to you. That is prophecy. It doesn't matter if you have ever received a prophetic word from someone else; you now have words of life at your disposal to wage war on the enemy and clear out the storms of life.

You may have wondered throughout our journey why I insist on writing things down. A written word is a tool of weaponry that counters the schemes of the enemy. Rereading and praying over your written exercises is a great way to remind yourself that you were created for a purpose, with an identity that fits that purpose, and that God isn't finished with you yet.

Paul wrote these words to his student Timothy,

> *Do not neglect the spiritual gift within you, which was bestowed on you through prophetic utterances with the laying on of hands by the presbytery. Take pains with these things; be absorbed in them, so that your progress will be evident to all* (1 Timothy 4:14–15).

Paul's advice is to use the prophetic words as reminders of the *so **much more*** that the Lord has for you. He is admonishing Timothy and you to remember and be absorbed in prophetic utterances, not to stick them in a drawer and forget about them. He is also NOT advising you to just let the Lord do all the work. Where the NASB Bible translation uses "be absorbed" in verse 15, other translations use words and phrases like practice, occupy, be diligent, meditate, and give complete attention. In other words, we are to actively use the prophetic wisdom and guidance that we receive from Heaven or from others to navigate through times of stillness and times of stress. The words you receive come with the promise of fulfillment. Keeping that promise front and center helps you stay on track as you navigate through turbulence.

Prophetic Promises

When God speaks a word, whether directly to you or through other people, it contains the power to accomplish what the word says. When Holy Spirit speaks encouragement, edification, or comfort about any area of your life, He will bring it to pass. The promise of Isaiah 55:11 assures us that God's word will not return to Him empty, without accomplishing what He desires, or without succeeding in the matter for which He sent it.

> *"For as the rain and the snow come down from heaven,*
> *And do not return there without watering the earth*
> *And making it bear and sprout,*
> *And furnishing seed to the sower, and bread to the eater;*
> *So will My word be which goes forth from My mouth;*
> *It will not return to Me empty,*
> *Without accomplishing what I desire,*
> *And without succeeding in the matter for which I sent it"*
> (Isaiah 55:10–11).

God's language is spirit language, and it is often poetic. There are times when it should not be interpreted literally. Be careful to hold loosely the interpretation and expectation of how things are going to look and/or when they are going to happen. However, if you have yet to see words from the Lord fulfilled in your life, it may be time to speak them out, to pray them in, and to remind yourself that they are God's truth. Prophetic words can also become a weapon used in our battle against the enemy.

Fight the Good Fight

Paul gave Timothy another valuable use of prophetic words when he wrote:

> *This command I entrust to you, Timothy my son, in accordance with the prophecies previously made concerning you, that by them you fight the good fight* (1 Timothy 1:18).

What does it mean to "fight the good fight" with prophecies? We must take authority over our circumstances by reminding ourselves and the powers of darkness of the future that the Lord has shown us through prophecy. This fighting with prophecy happened several years ago in a very real way for a close friend of mine. Her son was involved in a water-skiing accident. His neck was broken. He was emergency-flighted to Vanderbilt Hospital here in Nashville and was admitted into the intensive care trauma unit. It was more than 24 hours before they could get him into surgery. During that time, I told my friend to read and/or listen to all of the prophecies that had been spoken over him. They spoke of a future full of life and blessing. Not only were the prophecies a comfort for the family, they served to take a stand against anything that would come against his full recovery.

Reviewing those prophecies not only brought comfort and hope, but they also spoke life and helped the family stand against any scheme of the enemy. Remembering what God had said also enabled them to take any negative thought captive as they awaited surgery and went through the months of physical therapy. Every step in the healing process was a reminder of God's promises to this young man. I am happy to say that he did recover fully and he leads a very active and normal life. To this day, that family celebrates his recovery with numerous prayers of thanksgiving. Giving God thanks is another tried-and-true way to make it through the cloudy, foggy, and stormy seasons.

Give Thanks in Everything

I want to point out a difference in language that may seem small at first glance, but in fact, it is significant: the difference between advice that says give thanks FOR everything and one that says give thanks IN everything. IN implies that wherever you are, whatever you are facing, there is space to thank the Lord.

Be anxious for nothing, but in everything by prayer and supplication with thanksgiving let your requests be made known to God (Philippians 4:6).

The juxtaposition in Paul's instruction is worth noting. On the one hand, something seems to be causing enough anxiety that he is admonishing the Philippians to a) not be anxious, and b) take it to the Lord in prayer. In the middle, he says to bring it to the Lord with thanksgiving. It begs the question: What are people to be thankful for if they are struggling with something big enough to cause anxiety and seek the Lord? The answer is found in another passage penned by Paul.

Rejoice always; pray without ceasing; in everything give thanks; for this is God's will for you in Christ Jesus (1 Thessalonians 5:16–18).

Paul says that we are to give thanks IN everything. Philippians 4:6 doesn't say to give thanks FOR everything, but it does say IN everything. You don't need to thank the Lord FOR the storm you are in, but IN the midst of the storm, give Him thanks. Offerings of praise and thanksgiving to the Lord, even in the most dire circumstances, acknowledge that He alone is in charge and is sovereign. Bringing worship full of thanksgiving says, "I don't understand this, but I trust YOU, Lord, so I offer You thanks for what You are about to do in my life." It is a posture of humility and worship.

Thanking God in everything is an act of worship. It is praise. It is surrender, which brings peace in the midst of the chaos. It is why Paul goes on to tell the Philippians the result of bringing their anxiety to God with thanksgiving:

And the peace of God, which surpasses all comprehension, will guard your hearts and your minds in Christ Jesus (Philippians 4:7).

Not only does thanksgiving usher in miraculous peace, it also serves as a sentinel posted around your heart and mind to keep you in that place of peace. Being at peace means that you remain calm and mindful of God's Presence even when it seems like God has turned on the blender in your life. Fill your days with thanksgiving and watch as you stay in perfect peace. A thankful heart does not have room for doubt. A grateful heart ensures that you speak words of thanksgiving and life. Speaking life, light, and blessing is another tool that clears the storms.

Guard Your Tongue

What are you speaking over your life? When you find yourself battling discouragement, take a look at the words you are speaking about yourself and your life. Do you think your words don't matter? Consider the story of the fig tree that withered and died when Jesus cursed it (Matthew 21:18–22). If you think the tree died just because Jesus as the Son of God cursed it, remember that everything Jesus did, He did as fully man filled with the Holy Spirit. Because you carry the same Holy Spirit that Jesus did, your words would carry the same power to kill a fig tree if you were to curse it. In fact, Jesus tells us that as His followers we will do even more than He did.

> *Truly, truly, I say to you, he who believes in Me, the works that I do, he will do also; and greater works than these he will do; because I go to the Father* (John 14:12).

In addition, Jesus tells His disciples how important their words are in the following passage:

> *And Jesus answered and said to them, "Truly I say to you, if you have faith and do not doubt, you will not only do what was done to the fig tree, but even if you say to this mountain, 'Be taken up and cast into the sea,' it will happen"* (Matthew 21:21).

James 3:10 says that both blessing and cursing come from the same mouth. Speak blessing. Choose to speak life. Speak abundance and prosperity of mind, body, and spirit. One of my favorite passages of blessing to speak out loud is found in Psalm 103:

> *Bless the LORD, O my soul,*
> *And ALL that is within me, bless His Holy name.*
> *Bless the LORD, O my soul,*
> *And forget none of His benefits;*
> *Who pardons all your iniquities,*
> *Who heals all your diseases;*
> *Who redeems your life from the pit,*
> *Who crowns you with lovingkindness and compassion;*
> *Who satisfies your years with good things,*
> *So that your youth is renewed like the eagle* (Psalm 103:1–5).

There is no age limit on God's forgiveness, God's healing, or His redemption. There is no limit to His lovingkindness or compassion, so it stands to reason that He will bring satisfaction, good things, life, and renewal at any age. It is never too late to speak life, light, and blessing over your mind, body, spirit, and life. Speaking life can become difficult, however, when you find yourself in the midst of those who speak curses, death, darkness, and destruction.

Guard Your Heart

Look closely at your life's journey. Who are your traveling companions? When you feel vulnerable to the attacks of the enemy, being mindful about how you spend your time and with whom is critical. You already know the people in your life who stand with you in your hopes and dreams. You also know those who are skeptical at best or who the enemy is using to discourage you and cause you to question your dreams and visions.

It helps to remember that Jesus did not ask all 12 of the disciples to pray with Him in the Garden of Gethsemane on the night that He was betrayed. He asked those closest to Him: Peter, James, and John (Mark 14:33). When you are in the midst of a storm, feeling pushed from all sides, you need to heed the advice to guard your gifts, your heart, and your spirit from those who don't understand or stand with you.

Who are the cheerleaders in your life? Who are the listeners who encourage and support what God is doing in and through your life? Who will remind you of the words the Lord has spoken to you? Not only is it wise to stay away from the naysayers, but also it is helpful to spend a little more time with those who will keep you on your path.

Allow me to offer a word of caution here. Do not assume that those closest to you in relationship will be those who will encourage and support you. Jesus experienced this in Nazareth, His hometown. Even Jesus could not do many miracles when He returned to His hometown. What is true for Jesus, is often and unfortunately, true for the rest of us.

And they took offense at Him. But Jesus said to them, "A prophet is not without honor except in his hometown and in his own household" (Matthew 13:57).

If you find yourself battling discouragement and disappointment, take a look around you and check who is speaking into your life. At times, the only voice to heed is that of the Lord, your Audience of One. He is the One who created you, and the One who gave you your identity and your purpose. He is the One who knows the end from the beginning, and He knows in which direction you are soaring. Stay connected to Him and His voice, and you will stay on course through the storm.

Stay Connected

You stay connected to the Lord by planning, scheduling, and following through on time spent in His Presence and in His Word. If you take the time to abide with Him, you will stay connected to His plans and purposes for your life in spite of how your circumstances look.

You are not meant to walk out your destiny in a vacuum. As I have mentioned, surrounding yourself with those in your life who will speak life, light, and blessing is so important. This encircling process takes effort and requires attention. Spending the time to tend to spouses, children, parents, siblings, friends, and colleagues is critical, and relationships are important to the Lord. Jesus lived a life that exemplified the importance of relationship over religion. He often dined with His friends away from the ministry spotlight. Follow His example. Spend time with your spouse. Make time for your children. Honor your parents. Life goes by too quickly to assume that deep relationships will take place naturally. One of satan's schemes is to place wedges between family members, whether that is our bloodline family, our family in Christ, or our family in the marketplace. Guard and protect your relationships, especially those who God has clearly shown will link arms with you and assist you on your journey.

Staying connected also includes paying careful attention to the child within. If the storms of life feel oppressive, perhaps it is time to relax, recreate, and rejuvenate. We are all meant to have a childlike faith, but all too often, we mature right out of the joy and fun of this adventure we call life. Take vacations. Enjoy life. Relax. Take a nap. Read a good novel. Play like a child. There is time for work and there is time for play. Don't confuse the two.

As you stay connected to the Lord, He may show you areas of your life that are hindering your forward progress in your journey of purpose. It is always a good strategy to periodically ask, "Lord, is there something in my life that is blocking all that you have for me?"

Stay Clean Before the Lord

There are times when the Lord will slow progress to allow time to do heart business with Him. Harboring unforgiveness or living with unrepented sin can slow progress to a crawl or even a halt. Your character matters to God. It is foundational to what the Lord wants to do in your future. Ask the Lord to purify and wash your heart. The prayer of David in Psalm 51 applies to all as a way to stay clean before the Lord.

Create in me a clean heart, O God,
And renew a steadfast spirit within me.
Do not cast me away from Your presence
And do not take Your Holy Spirit from me.
Restore to me the joy of Your salvation
And sustain me with a willing spirit.
Then I will teach transgressors Your ways,
And sinners will be converted to You (Psalm 51:10–13).

Notice the emphasis on the word "then" in the phrase, "Then *I will teach transgressors Your ways.*" The emphasis is not mine; it is the Lord's. What that emphasis says to me is that God waits for us to clean our hearts before He releases us into the purposes He has given us. I repeat: **Character matters to God.** How we look at life, how we approach situations that arise also matter to God. Do you look at adversity through the eyes of self-pity? Self-pity is rooted in the poor-pitiful-me attitude that asks, "Why is this happening to me?" If you are too focused on the "why" of your stormy season, you may miss the lessons God has for you.

Change Your "Whys" to "Whats"

You won't necessarily understand God's plan or purpose when circumstances play out in your life differently than you had hoped or expected. God's ways are not our ways. His thoughts are higher than our thoughts (Isaiah 55:8–9). You may not understand, but you can count on His love and His faithfulness. You can bank on His promise that He will work all things together for your good when you love Him and are called according to His purpose (Romans 8:28). He has your best interest at heart. He is faithful to strengthen you when you run to Him. He is faithful to the call He has given you. It is His job to bring it to pass (1 Thessalonians 5:24).

Change your "Why?" question to "What can I learn?", "What do you want me to do?", or "How can I help someone else?" Asking "Why?" puts the focus on you and your life. "What" and "how" questions remove the poor-pitiful-me attitude and rids you of the evil spirit poised to take you down the slippery slope of despair into the pit of self-pity.

Lessons are always there to be learned. People are always there to be served. Work is always there to be done. Lessons, people, or work may be missed when you are searching for why the storm is hitting you. Focusing on "why" is like putting your life under a microscope. With eyes solely focused on what is seen through a small lens, anything else that is going on in the lab is missed. Perhaps the very thing you are waiting for is standing right next to you, but you can't see it because you have your head down, staring at the details of your circumstances. Look up from your self-focus and see what God has for you in the midst of the storm. Storms are inevitable. How you handle them is your choice.

Just as your identity and purpose are unique, so are the challenges that we face in life. Do not let others dictate the validity of your "storm season." All types of storms exist and some are more intense than others; some last longer than others. The truth is that storms are a part of life. It is, therefore, vitally important that we are prepared to face them and able to navigate through them as we soar with God on our flight path of purpose and destiny. The exercise for this chapter is one of recognition and preparation.

SOARING WITH GOD
Exercise 23: Storm Tracking
It's time to take out your notebook. Set aside some time to ask the Lord where you are in relationship to the storm track. This location exercise will allow you to heighten your awareness of the spiritual atmosphere in your life at the present time.

Here are some useful questions. Again, please write out your answers.

1. Are you in the midst of a storm? If so, what does it look like? What challenges do you face?
2. Are you coming out of a storm? Describe your recent season of challenges and how you faced them.
3. Do you see storm clouds brewing? Sometimes the Lord gives us hints that challenges are coming. I do not want you to look for something that is not there, but acknowledge what may be on the horizon.
4. Are you in a season of smooth sailing? That's awesome! Recognize it, treasure it, and give thanks.

Exercise 24: Tools of the Trade

Now that your radar is tuned to see where you are in relation to turbulence, go back through the chapter and ask Holy Spirit to show you which strategies would be best to help you navigate through this season and prepare you for the future. This side of Heaven, improvements can always be made in every one of the strategies I have listed. Ask Holy Spirit to show you which one(s) He is highlighting to prepare you for the future. As He highlights a strategy, ask Him for a specific way to apply that strategy in your life today. Ask the Lord for a plan to include these strategies and steps in your daily schedule. Write that plan down and commit to sticking to it.

1. **Prayer and Worship:** Have I set aside time daily to pray and acknowledge the Lord for who He is? Am I adhering to my schedule to meet with the Lord daily?

2. **Take Your Thoughts Captive:** Do I allow my negative thoughts to dictate my choices or do I silence them by taking them captive to the obedience of Christ? What Scriptures can I use to replace my negative thoughts?

3. **Be Absorbed:** Do I diligently remind myself of the future the Lord has shown me? Am I taking the step that the Lord has shown me needs to be taken today?

4. **Prophetic Promises:** What encouragements have I received from others and from the Lord? Am I praying over them regularly? Is there a prophetic promise that I need to write out and put where I can read it daily?

5. **Fight the Good Fight:** When spiritual attacks happen, do I use the promises of God to resist the enemy? Am I declaring God's plan for my life out loud?

6. **Give Thanks in Everything:** Do I live a life full of gratitude? Do I give Father, Son, and Holy Spirit thanks in whatever circumstances I find myself? In the midst of this particular storm, what is one thing I am thankful for?

7. **Guard Your Tongue:** What am I speaking over my life? Am I complaining about the storm I am experiencing, or am I declaring that I will overcome it and it will pass?

8. **Guard Your Heart:** Who are the cheerleaders in my life? How can I connect with one or more of these people? Who has shown interest in my project? Do I need to set up a lunch date with my encouragers?

9. **Stay Connected:** Is it time to take a vacation or to go on a date with my spouse? Do I need to join a Bible study group to deepen my connection with God and other believers? What can I do to fuel my passion for my God-given purpose?

10. **Stay Clean Before the Lord:** Is it time to set up an appointment with an inner healing ministry? Who do I need to forgive? When I spend time with God, for what do I need to ask forgiveness?

11. **Change your "Whys" to "Whats":** Do I need to repent of spending too much time asking the Lord why this storm is upon me? What can I learn from this storm? How can I serve others in the midst of my storm?

CELEBRATING YOUR PROGRESS AND MOVING FORWARD

Congratulations! You now carry a suitcase full of strategies for the air pockets, turbulence, or storms that you may face on your flight path. The Prince of Peace is your flying companion, and He is faithful to show you just how to use those strategies when the time arises. He is the source of the *so much more* peace that you now hold close to your heart. He also holds all of the navigational tools that you need to get through stormy seasons. Keep soaring with Him as you continue on this path of unlocking and releasing the *so much more* of who God created you to be and what He created you to do. God is the greatest strategist of all when it comes to unlocking all that He has for you. Next, we will put all the key strategies together to more easily help you soar with God along your flight path.

First, let's pray, worship, and give thanks together.

> Heavenly Father, storms in life are tough! Often there is no way around them, yet we know that You travel with us in the midst of the turbulent times in our lives. Would You bring peace in the midst of the storm as You remind us of these methods that will help us navigate the stormy times? We thank You that You never leave us or forsake us, and we are grateful that we can trust that Your Presence is with us every step of the way. In Jesus' name, Amen.

11.
Created For So Much More
STRATEGY:
Unlocking An Amazing Future

As I have traveled my own journey of redemption and renewal, the Lord has shown Himself to be the Breaker of Chains, the Destroyer of Lies, the Lover of My Soul, and *so much more*. As I have soared with God and coached others to do the same, He has faithfully and consistently provided nuggets of truth that I have collected and shared. It was as I prepared to host the first *Created For So Much More* conference that Holy Spirit showed me these nuggets were more than nice little truths. He clearly spoke that they were key strategies to unlock His desired future for His children. I was to take them seriously and share them generously.

These keys have been tested and are tried and true. Some you will recognize from previous chapters because I consider them so important that they warranted expanded attention earlier in the book. They continue to be forged and refined through the seasons of my life. These keys are truths that I have shared through hours of counsel and mentoring. Other people find them as valuable as I do. Here I present them together on a key ring of sorts. By gathering them together in one place, I offer an easy reference guide to keep handy. These keys are meant to be used regularly in your life. They are critical for unlocking the amazing *so much more* that the Lord has for you. I am confident that these keys will unlock your identity, your purpose and destiny, and your future. Don't take my word for it. Use them. Take one out and try it for a while. See the difference it makes. The first three strategies are the master keys. They are the most important and the broadest of the set. Although I could have included the remaining keys as a part of the first three, I believe they are each important enough to be recognized individually. The whole idea of having keys of truth to unlock your future implies that you have a choice about whether or not to use them. That choice is where our ring of key strategies to unlock your amazing future begins.

1. Take Responsibility

The poor-pitiful-me syndrome is rampant in the body of Christ. "If only I could do that." "If only that hadn't happened to me as a child." "If only I had the kind of job he has." The list goes on. These self-pity statements may even sound like they are spiritual: "If only I knew Scripture like she does." "If only I heard from God like he does." Can I just say it? All of these statements are nonsense. You are responsible for living your life. You are responsible for the decisions that you make and the steps that you take on this journey. You make a choice to be an overcomer or a victim. You choose: how you use your 24 hours each day, who spends time with you, and what you speak over your life and your family. You have a choice to wallow in the things of the past or to allow King Jesus to redeem and restore that which the enemy has stolen.

Remember, sometimes you need more than prayer. Sometimes you need to change your decisions. Life happens and we face an enemy that does what he can to hurt, harm, and hinder the children of God. Jesus died and rose from the dead to give you the victory over sin, death, and the power of the devil. That means you can choose Jesus and abundant life—or not. Take responsibility for your choices and choose life. Some of the most important decisions you must make to unlock your future are to decide whom you will listen to and whose directions you follow. Those choices are part of the next key.

2. Play to the Audience of One

We all play to some kind of audience. Either you play to the voices that bring bondage and speak lies, or you play to the Audience of One, the Lord and Lover of your soul. The Greek chorus in your head that sings the praises of "should," insisting that "you should do this," or "you should do that," is not of God. You don't have the time or the energy to follow the "should do" list if you are to unlock your destiny. "Should" is a judgment word. Change your "should" to "I'd like to," and see what a difference that thought change makes. Your Audience of One does not judge you—He invites you to walk with Him to unlock *so much more.*

Listen only to the voice of The One who created you. I am not saying to disengage from those around you. I am saying that what the Lord speaks to you is far more important than what anyone else thinks. Your Audience of One may show you big audacious dreams and call you to a vision and mission that seems beyond yourself. That call to dream is significant and leads to the next key.

3. Dream Big, Work Small

We serve a big audacious God, and He has big audacious dreams for His children. Jesus said in John 10:10 that He came that we would have life and have it abundantly. Just before those words, however, He warns against the enemy who comes to steal, kill, and destroy. The enemy particularly loves to decimate the dreams of God's children. If your dream can come to pass through your own strength and abilities, then your dream is too small. Think big thoughts, Dear One. Dream big dreams!

The second part of this key strategy is just as important as dreaming big dreams. It says: Work Small. In other words, leave the work of unfolding your big dreams into reality to the Lord.

Think of it this way: You are on a path. You can glance up at the horizon, but if you focus there too long, you may stumble and fall. Watch your steps and let the Lord take care of where the path leads. Let the Lord show you the direction of your step, the length of your stride, and the pace of your gait. How do you know where your next step should be? You use the next key on your ring, which is to stay connected.

4. Stay Connected

This key is all about staying connected to your passion, your tribe, your family, and your God. Staying connected includes engaging in habits and activities that bring you joy. Some of these activities are spiritually oriented—others are not. Choose to participate in those things that help you be who you were created to be and do what you were created to do. As you remain engaged, be mindful of your identity and purpose. Stay connected to the passionate child within who dreams big dreams. Along the way, you will discover that God is throwing bread crumbs along your path to guide you exactly where He wants you to go. Learning to recognize and interpret these signs is so important for your journey into the *so much more*. That's why reading the signs is the next key in your collection.

5. Read the Signs

Gideon was clear both when he put out a fleece and asked the Lord to make it wet (Judges 6:37) and when he later asked that everything else be wet except the fleece (Judges 6:39). God answered Gideon exactly as he requested. God didn't admonish Gideon for asking for a sign—instead the Lord gave Gideon one.

The Lord uses things around you to speak to you in the same way He spoke to Gideon. He will use everyday things in your life to point you in the direction that He is asking you to go. Ask Him for wisdom and discernment, in addition to revelation and knowledge, not only to see the signs themselves but also to read and comprehend His message. Peace is a powerful sign. Sensitize your spirit to become aware of Heaven's peace and watch for other signposts along the road. Like a traffic light, these signs will show you the way.

Lean in to the Presence of God and rest, knowing that He is trustworthy and that He will bring you signs and peace for your future. He is also faithful to show you your unique flight plan, but it is your job to follow the singular path that the Lord presents to you. This is the next key.

6. Follow Your Path

You possess a gift mix and personality profile that is uniquely yours. Why then, Dear One, do you look to the right or to the left and compare your life to someone else's? I know that I'm repeating myself here, but this principle is important to remember: **No one else carries the exact purpose for which you were created.** At times, you will have companionship on your path, but sometimes you will feel very lonely. When you find yourself alone in your journey, trust the Lord's words spoken through Jeremiah to the exiled leaders of Israel.

> *'For I know the plans that I have for you,' declares the Lord, 'plans for welfare and not for calamity to give you a future and a hope. Then you will call upon Me and come and pray to Me, and I will listen to you. You will seek Me and find Me when you search for Me with all your heart. I will be found by you,' declares the Lord, 'and I will restore your fortunes and will gather you from all the nations and from all the places where I have driven you,' declares the Lord, 'and I will bring you back to the place from where I sent you into exile'* (Jeremiah 29:11–14).

There are so many promises in this passage!
1. Your future is known by God.
2. Your future is full of hope.
3. When you call on the Lord, He listens.
4. When you seek Him, He will be found.
5. Your fortunes will be restored.

6. You will not remain alone on your path—even though it may feel like exile.

Trust the Lord's wisdom and guidance, take His hand, and keep walking. Continuing to walk forward is the next key on your key ring of strategies that unlock your amazing future.

7. Keep Walking

Keep walking—no matter what. Put one foot in front of the other, moving forward each and every day. Some days, you will have a difficult time seeing where you are going. At those times, grab hold of the hand of the One who walks with you, and keep walking. Some days, you won't get very far along your path, and other days you will be out of breath because of the distance that you have run. The Lord knows where you are going and exactly what time you need to arrive at your destination. You may not see it, but He does. His perspective is perfect. God moves on your behalf, even when you feel like you are standing still.

You may find yourself in times and seasons when it is difficult to see where to take the next step. The next key is always a good one to use in moments when you are stumped over the next goal or agenda item.

8. Hone Your Skills

Keeping your skills honed and ready to use is necessary to unlock the *so much more* version of who you were created to be and what you were created to do. Staying in a posture of learning is what keeps you flexible before the Lord and usable for His purposes. God pours *so much more* of Himself into you when you open yourself to receive training and improvement. Consistently seek ways to improve in all that you do in order to reach a higher standard of excellence.

Michael Port, a speaker, trainer, and *New York Times* best-selling author of *Steal the Show*, says that the worst speakers can be those who are natural communicators because they tend to rely on their natural abilities, rather than to educate, train, and push themselves to be extraordinary speakers.[24] Don't settle for ordinary. Don't be content with the status quo. Hone your skills to become extraordinary.

Holy Spirit is committed to your dream. Holy Spirit is there to help you move forward in your destiny, and Holy Spirit is capable of teaching you all that you need to know to accomplish whatever God is asking of you. Honing your skills means creating learning experiences even if public opportunities don't arise. Don't wait for the big break to happen. Don't wait until you "feel" like it. Don't wait until things are safe or until everything comes together in a neat, tidy package. If your vision is to be a writer, but publishers aren't knocking on your door, consider writing a newsletter, a blog, or beginning your book. Are you called to preach, yet have no invitations to speak? Write your message and then preach to your cat or an empty room, or while you are driving. Learning and practicing isn't striving; it is co-laboring with Holy Spirit. Working on your craft leads to the next key for unlocking your future. You must be willing and able to do whatever is necessary. Sometimes what needs doing is less than glamorous. Sometimes it is just plain hard work—the next key.

9. Do The Work

Doing the work unlocks opportunity, divine appointments, and an amazing future. It also is the way to defeat opposition that arises. Steven Pressfield, author of *Do the Work*, says that resistance will attack us every time we begin to step out in our creativity, our self-improvement, or our attempts to change the world. In his words, "Any act that rejects immediate gratification in favor of long-term growth, health, or integrity" or "any act that derives from our higher nature instead of our lower" will hit resistance.[25] The only way around the resistance is to do the work.

Masters in any field put in whatever time it takes. Both artists and athletes do the mundane tasks required to keep their minds, bodies, and spirits in peak condition, ready for the next performance, project, or sporting event. Play your scales, lift your weights, read, write, and study. Do that thing that you don't like to do, but that you know is important. You will reap the reward if you sow time and effort into the work.

Scripture tells us in Zechariah 4:10 to not despise the day of small things or small beginnings. Doing the work can feel like a small thing. Often it is not fun or comfortable. Doing the work may mean that you need to stop postponing and actually invest the time it takes to learn new technology. It might mean cold-calling potential clients. Perhaps it is doing the accounting work, writing a business/ministry plan, or setting goals. As a professional artist, I spend as much time marketing, bookkeeping, photographing, framing, etc. as I do painting a canvas. That, my friends, is doing the work. Some of it is not as enjoyable as painting a canvas, but it is necessary.

Another aspect of doing the work is serving others, especially those who God has put in your path and those who may have much to teach you. Be willing to jump into the fray, get your hands dirty, and your feet wet. Serve where you are asked to serve. Doing the work is a part of a contented life. Being content to do what needs doing today leads us to the next key in our ring of strategies.

10. Live Now

As you do the work of today without longingly gazing at the future or at others' successes, you engage in the strategy to live now. Living now connects somewhat to the "Dream Big, Work Small" key in that you focus and live each day as it comes, being content to work small. Jesus tells us in Matthew's Gospel, *"Do not worry about tomorrow; for tomorrow will care for itself"* (Matthew 6:34). Who has God put in your path today? A mundane meeting can transform into a major opportunity in the Lord's hands.

Learn to be content wherever you are. This learning process is part of the push/pull of faith. Live with big dreams within you, and you will undoubtedly live with a certain amount of tension. Years ago, the Lord showed me that this tension was holy discontentment. You feel it when the Lord uses "uncomfortableness" to keep you from complacency. Holy discontentment keeps you investigating, studying, and moving forward in the things that He calls you to do.

You must not long so much for the future, even the future of Heaven or Christ's return, that you do not take up the task at hand. Your job is to reach for the *so much more* of God while living and soaring in the space and time of today.

Even in the space of daily work, soaring can be exhilarating. As I work from the screened-in porch overlooking the Florida mangroves, I have a perfect view of ospreys, hawks, and vultures soaring on the wind currents in the skies that surround me. Watching them is inspirational. The heights and dips of flight mimic a ride on a roller coaster. If I were to imagine myself soaring like an eagle, it would seem a little risky. Similarly, soaring with God may feel a little risky—which brings us to the next key in our collection.

11. Take Risks

If you are to experience the *so much more* of God and the amazing life He has for you, it will require you to take risks. The more time I have been walking with the Lord, the more I have found that life in the Lord or living by the Spirit is quite an adventure! If you are bored with the life you are leading,

I would go so far as to say you that aren't fully living in your God-given identity. I have never known the Lord to be boring. Certainly there are times of rest, but overall, those I know who fully embrace living in the Spirit speak of the roller-coaster life they lead. It is a life full of ups and downs, twists and turns, adventure and fun.

God is not in a box. He doesn't put His children in boxes either. Get used to living outside the box of normal living. Get used to being uncomfortable and being placed outside your comfort zone. Trust the Lord that when He says *"Leap,"* either the net will appear or He will give you wings to fly. At times, the Lord will say *"wait"* just as you are ready to leap. Those waiting activities can be the riskiest of all. They require strength and courage. The Lord knows you better than you know yourself. Although you may face risks, the Lord will not ask you to do anything that does not fit His plan and purpose for your life or who He created you to be.

He wants you to live authentically in the identity He gave you. Living a life that reflects who you are brings us to the last strategic key to use as you soar with God and unlock the *so **much more*** that He has for you.

12. Live Your Message

What is your life message? How does your life reflect that message? What do your words and actions tell others about you and the God you serve? Do you walk your talk?

If you have an at-home business, it is easy to work in pajamas, unshowered, with coffee in hand and crumbs falling everywhere around the computer. However, it isn't the best strategy to set you up for success. I recently heard an online entrepreneur say that she works like a rock star when she is dressed like a rock star. What she was saying was that she accomplished more when she took the time to clean up, dress professionally, and approach her at-home business with the same attitude that she would if she were going to an office. Living your message builds the same kind of self-confidence, credibility, and authority.

We all wear different "hats" in our life. I am wife, mother, grandmother, speaker, artist, minister, daughter, sister, and coach. I am always all of those, although I will bring out certain elements at different times, depending on the situation. I think of the various aspects of my life like sections of instruments in a symphony orchestra. As the conductor of my life, I play sounds at various decibels so that they will be heard differently at different times. As the conductor, I am also responsible for bringing all of the instruments together to perform one piece of music in beautiful harmony. Despite the various combinations of sounds, the music of my life should sound like the same orchestra is playing day after day. That's walking the talk and living my message.

Now that you hold these keys in your hand, how do you know when to use which one? That is the focus on our next exercise.

Keys = Strategies

I have intentionally used the terms keys and strategies interchangeably throughout this chapter because each of the 12 points is a key strategy that I have used successfully in my own life and in coaching others. This next exercise has been another favorite at my conferences. At first blush, it seems one-dimensional, but I promise there is great depth of understanding to be gained as you work through this next step. God will reveal *so **much more*** of Himself and how much more He wants to unlock in your life.

SOARING WITH GOD

Exercise 25: Which Strategies?

Do you know how your muscles get stronger? Resistance training, which happens when you lift weights, builds muscle. Exercising your spiritual man is no different. When snags or resistance surface, the Lord may be saying, *"Let's work on this."* As we come to the end of our journey together, I want to review the 12 key strategies that will unlock your amazing future.

Grab your notebook or journal. As you read and copy each key from the following list in your own handwriting, ask the Lord to reveal how that key pertains to your life or what He wants to highlight to you. Ask for the wisdom and guidance to learn how to take hold of that key, insert it in the lock and open the doorway to your future.

Please do not race through this exercise. Pray through each key, whether the Lord has highlighted it or not. We are never operating at 100 percent with these keys; some will need work today and others will need work tomorrow or next week. By praying through each key, and asking yourself the corresponding questions, these truths will become more ingrained in your spirit, making them easier to remember and use.

1. **Take Responsibility.** What choices am I making?
2. **Play to the Audience of One.** To whom do I listen for my life's decisions?

3. **Dream Big, Work Small.** Do I have big audacious dreams and am I taking small steps to accomplish them?

4. **Stay Connected.** Am I putting forth effort to stay in touch with God, family, friends, as well as my inner self?

5. **Read the Signs.** What signposts have I noticed along my path? What do they say to me?

6. **Follow Your Path.** Am I staying on the course the Lord has set for me, or am I getting distracted by others?

7. **Keep Walking.** Have challenges stalled me, or am I continuing to walk at whatever pace the Lord leads?

8. **Hone Your Skills.** What area of my gifts and talents could be improved?

9. **Do the Work.** Have I neglected the nitty-gritty tasks associated with my big dream?

10. **Live Now.** Am I living a contented life?

11. **Take Risks.** Have I let fear or anxiety keep me from taking the next step that the Lord has for me to take?

12. **Live Your Message.** Does my life exemplify my beliefs, character, and passion?

Exercise 26: Your Personal Strategies

Perhaps while you've been reading this list of key strategies, Holy Spirit has whispered other keys that He has given you for your life and your future. We all carry our own unique sets of keys. Perhaps you have keys hanging on your key ring that look different than mine. What are your life lessons? Which truths has the Lord highlighted as "words to live by"?

Write them in your notebook or journal, creating a new section, like this one.

MY PERSONAL STRATEGIES TO UNLOCK MY FUTURE:

1.

2.

3.

4.

5.

CELEBRATING YOUR PROGRESS AND MOVING FORWARD

Keys come in all shapes and sizes, and they serve many purposes. They open doors, start engines, and unlock safes that contain hidden treasures. Your strategies are keys that unlock the amazing future the Lord has for you. Keep them handy, and continue to ask the Lord which key is needed to unlock the door that leads to your future. Seek Him about which one to use to start the engine that will propel you into your destiny. Sit in His Presence to unlock the safe that contains the hidden treasure of the *so much more* that God has for you. I know that the keys that I have shared work. I have experienced their effectiveness in my own life and in the lives of those I coach. Put them into action and see what the Lord does on your behalf.

Congratulations! You have done the work necessary to take flight. Dear One, I can't tell you how proud I am that you have walked this far in your journey with the Lord! I know He has great things planned for you. We have one last stop together. Are you ready to soar with God into your amazing future?

Before we take flight, allow me to pray and give thanks for all the Lord has done.

> Father, Jesus, and Holy Spirit, thank You for all of the time that we have spent together on our journey of discovering the *so much more* that You have for each and every one of Your flock. You are the Way, the Truth, and the Life. We thank You for showing the way to *so much more* strategy. We express gratitude and praise for the nuggets of truth that You have given us as keys to help us unlock our future. We look forward to a life filled with Your empowering Presence, enabling us to be who You created us to be and to do what You created us to do. Pour out your Spirit as we move forward in our journey to take flight. In Jesus' name. Amen.

12.
Created For So Much More
FLIGHT:
Changing Atmospheres

"Are we there yet?" What parent has not heard that question over and over again. In fact, I am guilty of asking that question mid-flight on many journeys. As we travel from one place to the other here on Earth, we have set destinations. In the spiritual realm, there are no set destinations. The answer to the question, "Are we there yet?" for our purposes, is always "NO"—this side of eternity. Soaring with God means that our destinations are more stopovers than final arrivals. The arrival at one destination is the departure point for another part of life's adventure. Every day is an opportunity to take flight into the *so much more* that God has for you. Discovering the *so much more* of God and the *so much more* of who He created you to be and what He created you to do is a never-ending journey.

There is always more to discover about God, more to discover about your identity, more to discover about your purpose, and more to be done to change the world—one day at a time. Paul speaks of this journey when he writes to the Philippians about his own life of ministry.

"Not that I have already obtained it or have already become perfect, but I press on so that I may lay hold of that for which also I was laid hold of by Christ Jesus. Brethren, I do not regard myself as having laid hold of it yet; but one thing I do: forgetting what lies behind and reaching forward to what lies ahead, I press on toward the goal for the prize of the upward call of God in Christ Jesus" (Philippians 3:12–14).

There is always more Kingdom purpose and Kingdom destiny. If we believe that we are being transformed daily more and more into the image of Christ (2 Corinthians 3:18), the work is never done. We should, like Paul, always be pressing on toward the prize of the upward call of God. We should adopt a life view that recognizes God's hand in bringing new things into our lives.

"If anyone is in Christ, he is a new creature; the old things passed away; behold new things have come" (2 Corinthians 5:17).

When you take this approach, your finish line automatically becomes your starting line. By now I hope you know deep in your being that you are uniquely and wonderfully made. Just in case it hasn't sunk in yet, I'll tell you again: The Lord has a future and a hope for you (Jeremiah 29:11). No matter your age or situation, God is in the business of declaring and doing new things. It is the enemy that says otherwise.

Let me remind you, the enemy of your soul would like you to believe that you are too young or too old, too educated, not educated enough, too poor, too needy, or too scared to do what is stirring in your spirit. The world will tell you many of the same things.

I see an army, camped in a valley. The enemy surrounds the army on the hillsides, threatening its existence. The people in the army sit by campfires. They worry and whisper, "What are we going to do?" They pray for wisdom and guidance. They worship the Lord, believing He will come through for them. All while they continue to sit around their campfires. The surrounding enemy grows bolder. It taunts and threatens them. The atmosphere is one of fear and intimidation, of defeat and worry. Holy Spirit brought that image of the army and the enemy to my mind just this morning. As I write, I am reminded of the Philistine Goliath's intimidation of the Children of Israel.

"When Saul and all Israel heard these words of the Philistine, they were dismayed and greatly afraid" (1 Samuel 17:11).

Meanwhile, out in the fields, David tended sheep. He had already been anointed king, but he was content to tend the sheep of his father. He was also satisfied to take supplies to his brothers in the army.

David's response to the taunting of the Philistine army is telling:

"Then David said to the Philistine, 'You come to me with a sword, a spear, and a javelin, but I come to you in the name of the LORD of hosts, the God of the armies of Israel, whom you have taunted. This day the LORD will deliver you up into my hands, and I will strike you down and remove your head from you. And I will give the dead bodies of the army of the Philistines this day to the birds of the sky and the wild beasts

of the earth, that all the earth may know that there is a God in Israel' "
(1 Samuel 17:45–46).

This is David the shepherd and David the musician and poet. This is Jesse's disregarded youngest son, who was small in stature and gentle in spirit. That description hardly lines up with the person who prophesies and delivers a grizzly death to Goliath the Philistine. What can't be overlooked is that David knew the Lord. David understood the *so much more* of God. He had dedicated himself to doing what God asked of him right where he was. To David, the Philistine's taunts were not directed at the Israelites, but at the Lord. That was something he would not tolerate. What David does next is a lesson for us all.

David refused the armor offered to him by Saul (1 Samuel 17:39) Instead, he takes his stick, his sling, and his shepherd's bag. To his bag, he adds five smooth stones from a nearby brook. David uses the tools of his trade as a shepherd that were also available to him in the moment of the battle to defeat Israel's enemy. Wow!

God uses men and women who, like David, dedicate themselves to being excellent at what they do—right where they live. God empowers those who are more concerned with bringing glory to God than glory to themselves. God strengthens and preserves those who seek and know the *so much more* of who He is. God uses men and women right where they are, with the tools of their trade, to advance His kingdom, defeat the enemy, and change the world.

Putting on the Purposes of God

I see an army, encamped in a valley, sitting complacently around campfires. But I also see that army rising up to take the land, right where each person awakens to the *so much more* of God and the *so much more* that He has for each individual. As the army stands up, ready to serve, each person receives the mantle given by the Creator. As each man, woman, and child recognizes the gifts given by the Creator, custom-made uniforms are fitted like gloves. We are members of this army! As we acknowledge and begin to operate in the purpose for which we were created, we change the atmosphere where we live. As the spiritual atmosphere changes, the Kingdom of God advances, and territory that has been stolen by the enemy of our souls is taken back.

You, as a part of God's army, were created for *so much more!* You were created to take the land right where you live—during your lifetime. You were created to change the world—whatever you do. You have spheres of influence, lives that you alone touch, and people you singularly come in contact with on a regular basis. Each time you interact with your world, you have the opportunity to affect it. You are a child of the Most High God. You were created to inspire, to lead, and to influence. You were created to bring His Presence into your world. You were created to change atmospheres and change the world as only you can.

You are a God-carrier. As you realize and embrace the *so much more* of Father, Son, and Holy Spirit, They become *so much more* a part of you. Their Presence is noticeable in your countenance. Their perspective becomes obvious in your speech and actions. You change the atmosphere by filling your mind, body, and spirit with the *so much more* of God. As you breathe in the Breath of Life that comes from Heaven, you become all that the Lord has for you to be and to do. You may be thinking that is easier said than done when you face daily schedules and deadlines that seem to interfere with quieting your spirit to receive the *so much more* of God. Our last exercise offers help to center you with the Lord any time of day.

SOARING WITH GOD

I have found two Scriptures to be perfect antidotes to the distractions that come our way in this journey of life. Both seem to be complete in their ability to hit the mark for anything that may be going on in life. I have spoken them to myself in all kinds of situations from riding on the subway to praying for my father in the middle of the night as he drew closer to the day he went to Heaven. I have used them out loud with clients and have seen these Scriptures shatter bondages to bring freedom. If these are the only two prayers you pray, you will find that they are enough.

The Lord's Prayer and The 23rd Psalm are like a powerful prescription that has the potential to bring miraculous healing, That's why I call these passages PreScriptures—they have the potential to bring miracles into your life. Take as needed, at least once daily. Take them alone or with others. They are powerful tools to release *so much more* of God's empowering Presence in your life, enabling you to be who He created you to be and to do what He created you to do.

Exercise 27: The Lord's Prayer
I have heard that it takes less than 30 seconds to say The Lord's Prayer. I've

also timed it. That's not a lot of time for such a powerful prayer. Let's pray it together in the words the Lord spoke to His disciples.

'Our Father, who is in heaven,
Hallowed be Your name.
'Your kingdom come,
Your will be done,
On earth as it is in heaven.
'Give us this day our daily bread.
'And forgive us our debts, as we also have forgiven our debtors.
'And do not lead us into temptation, but deliver us from evil. [For Yours
is the kingdom and the power and the glory forever. Amen.]
(Matthew 6:9–13).

Exercise 28: The 23rd Psalm

It was during an inner-healing appointment with a young lady who did not want me to pray for her that the Holy Spirit first showed me the power of The 23rd Psalm. She was comfortable with us "praying" this familiar psalm, and as we did, my eyes were open to the truth that these words, offered as a prayer, cover almost anything the world or satan can throw at us. Pair it with the Lord's Prayer and you will change the atmosphere surrounding you wherever you are.

The LORD is my shepherd,
I shall not want.
He makes me lie down in green pastures;
He leads me beside quiet waters,
He restores my soul;
He guides me in the paths of righteousness
For His name's sake.

Even though I walk through the valley of the shadow of death,
I fear no evil, for You are with me;
Your rod and Your staff, they comfort me.
You prepare a table before me in the presence of my enemies;
You have anointed my head with oil;
My cup overflows.
Surely goodness and lovingkindness will follow me all the days of my life,
And I will dwell in the house of the LORD forever (Psalm 23:1–6).

We come full circle in our journey of discovery. I began this book talking about affecting change—I end our journey together talking about changing atmospheres. You, Dear One, hold the power to change atmospheres! As you carry more of God in and with you, His Light is carried into the darkness. When the Light of Jesus is present, the darkness must flee and the atmosphere changes for Kingdom purposes. This entire book has been based on my belief that we, the Children of God, have the power to change the world as we embrace the *so much more* of God. Let us each harness and release His power and change the world's atmosphere. As we do so, we more fully become the people He created each of us to be, and we live more fully doing what He created each of us to do. I exhort you to continually engage in discovering the *so much more* of God and the *so much more* that He has for you. The journey is never over. **There is always *so much more!***

My final words to you are not so much a prayer as a prophetic declaration from Heaven:

> Arise, children of the Lord!
> Take flight, army of the Most High King!
> Soar with God in the strategic place where you live!
> Take the land for the King and the Kingdom of God.
> As you spread your wings and soar, you influence the culture.
> As you follow your unique flight plan, you change the world—
> one touch, one word, one life at a time.
> Take flight in the *so much more* of who you were created to be and in what you were created to do!
> Yours is a life full of hope and promise!
> Yours is a life of vision and intimacy!
> Yours is a life of adventure and risks
> and the *so much more* of God.
> Take Flight!
> Now is the time!
> This is the place!
> To God be all honor and glory forever and ever!
> Amen and Amen, it shall be so!

Hallelujah!

NOTES

1. **Created For So Much More Purpose**

2. **Created For So Much More Freedom**

   1"James Ryle," accessed March 14, 2017, www.truthworks.org.

3. **Created For So Much More Clarity**

4. **Created For So Much More Intimacy**

   2Merriam-Webster Online, s.v. "contender," accessed February 16, 2017, https://www.merriam-webster.com/dictionary/contender.

   3"Albert Einstein>Quotes>Quotable Quotes," goodreads.com, accessed February 16, 2017, http://www.goodreads.com/quotes/282814-the-most-beautiful-thing-we-can-experience-is-the-mysterious.

   4Chambers, Oswald, *My Utmost For His Highest,* ed. James Reimann (Grand Rapids: 1992).

5. **Created For So Much More Certainty**

   5Dr. Jeff Sanders, "The Story Behind "O Holy Night," *A Moment in History with Jeff Sanders* (blog), accessed February 16, 2017, http://www.aproundtable.org/history-blog/blog.cfm?ID=876&AUTHOR_ID=9.

6. **Created For So Much More Identity**

   6"About I am Second," I Am Second, accessed February 16, 2017, http://www.iamsecond.com/about/.

7. **Created For So Much More Vision**

   7Shane Willard Ministries, "Positioned to Win," *Taking Responsibility,* God Aware DVD, accessed February 16, 2017, https://vimeo.com/ondemand/positionedtowin/193478057.

   8"Martin Luther Quotes," BrainyQuotes, accessed February 16, 2017, https://www.brainyquote.com/quotes/quotes/m/martinluth380369. html.

[9]"Pablo Picasso Quotes," BrainyQuotes, accessed February 16, 2017, https://www.brainyquote.com/quotes/quotes/p/pablopicas104106. html.

[10]"Wendy's Kitchen" ©Jim Gamble, accessed February 16, 2017, http://www.jimgamblestoryteller.com. Used with permission.

[11]*The American Heritage Dictionary of the English Language*, 1[st]ed., s.v. "similar."

[12]Seth Godin, *The Dip* (London, England: Portfolio, 2007), 10.

[13]"Ralph Waldo Emerson Quotes," BrainyQuotes, accessed March 7, 2017, https://www.brainyquote.com/quotes/quotes/r/ralphwaldo101322. html.

[14]Julia Cameron, *The Artist's Way* (New York: G.P. Putnam's Sons, 1992).

[15]Seth Godin. *Purple Cow* (London: Portfolio, 2002), 82.

[16]T.D. Jakes, *Destiny* (New York: FaithWords, Hachette Book Group, 2015), 207.

8. Created For So Much More Understanding

[17]Teasi Cannon, *My Big Bottom Blessing* (Brentwood: Worthy Publishing, 2012).

[18]James Strong, S.T.D., L.T.D., *The Exhaustive Concordance of the Bible* (Peabody: Hendrickson Publishing, 1890) 1102, #6960, 102.

[19]Ibid, 18, #6862, 101.

[20]Ibid, 19, #3905, 59.

[21]James Strong, S.T.D., L.T.D., *The Exhaustive Concordance of the Bible* (Peabody: Hendrickson Publishing, 1890) 47, #3956, 56.

9. Created For So Much More Rest

[22]Jonathan Cahn, *The Book of Mysteries* (Lake Mary: Charisma Media; Charisma House Book Group, 2016), Day 8.

[23]Jack Wellman, "What is Shekinah Glory? Is this in the Bible?" *Christian Crier* (blog: Patheos), accessed February 17, 2017, http://www.patheos.com/blogs/christiancrier/2014/05/17/what-is-shekinah-glory-is-this-in-the-bible/.

10. Created For So Much More Peace

11. Created For So Much More Strategy

[24]Michael Port, *Steal the Show* (New York: Houghton Mifflin Harcourt Publishing Corporation, 2015).

[25]Steven Pressfield. *Do the Work* (United States: Do Your Zoom, Inc., 2011), 5.

12. Created For So Much More Flight

ACKNOWLEDGEMENTS

First and foremost, I must give thanks to the Lord from whom everything else flows. He has shown me who He created me to be, redeemed my identity, and set me free. Through the inspiration and mandate to write this book, He gave me wings to fly in all that He created me to do. My gratitude knows no bounds.

To you the reader, thank you for taking the time and energy to read this book and do the exercises provided. You are a gift from God to me and to the world. Thank you for allowing me to guide you on this journey called life.

Without conferences or retreats, there would not be any material to put into print. A huge thank you to Lisa, Danyalle, Larry, Byron, Beth, Sara, Vertie, Sue, and Annaleigh, who have hosted and/or assisted with gatherings. Much of this material developed because you offered me a place to speak and share it. To the many volunteers of all of the conferences, I cannot thank you enough. You gave me the freedom to focus on teaching and ministering.

To the numerous people who have attended my conferences or given me the privilege to speak and minister during the past decades, thank you! It is through sharing your lives and stories that the Lord showed me that His Presence abides in the material compiled within these pages. You are the ones who have tested the exercises and given your stamp of approval. Specifically, I want to thank those who wrote testimonies: Lori, Melinda, Vertie, Beth, Danyalle, Zelena, Seth, Loral, Lisa Marie, Lynn, Lisa, and Anonymous. Your words throughout the last years have strengthened my resolve to keep going.

My team of intercessors has lifted me before the Lord for years. Your prayers are truly the wind beneath my wings! Thank you to Danyalle, Lisa, John, Jim, Barb, Melinda, Zelena, Inger, Juliet, Annaleigh, Beth, Loral, Teasi, Denny, and Amy who stood on the wall and prayed the prayers needed to bring this project to fruition.

To Scotti, Danyalle, Juliet, and Amy who read my very first draft and gave me the encouragement to continue the work of moving forward with this book—Thank you all! To Jim Gamble who played *Wendy's Kitchen* one day while we were chatting on the phone—what a treasure you are!

To my editor, Loral from Cowriterpro Editorial Services, you are a true silversmith. You took the raw material of my words, placed them in the refiner's fire of the editing process, and polished them to shine with the Presence of God. Thank you for stretching me as I transitioned this material from spoken word to written word. There is no doubt that this book is better because your gift and talent were applied to it.

To Kayla from Selah Press, thank you for your immediate enthusiasm and dedication to this project. Your publishing and design expertise, attention to detail, and standard of excellence were obvious from our first meeting. Thank you for taking this project over the finish line. What a joy!

To Victoria, thank you for the creativity and intricate skill that you applied to design a cover so well-suited to not only my cover painting but also to the content of the book.

To Lisa, my sweet friend, sister in Christ, prayer partner, assistant, and the voice of the Lord more often than not. You have walked with me from the conception of the first conference through the birthing of this book. You are the best sounding board an author could have. Your words always drip with the Presence of God, whether you are encouraging me or challenging me. Thank you! You have steadied me more times than you know.

I believe no writer completes a book without family support and encouragement. So, to Mom and Dad who passed down the gift and desire to teach, thank you! Dad, you lived a life on Earth doing what God created you to do and I am sure you are doing the same in Heaven. Your desire to "present the Gospel well" lives on! Mom, our time together and your thoughts for the back cover text and first chapters were priceless. At age 88, you are a shining example that God always has *so **much more*** for us.

To Frank and Amelia, the experience of fishing in the Gulf of Mexico with you brought fresh understanding to the Gospel, to Simon Peter, and the many fishing stories in the Bible. Thank you!

To Kim, your prayers, questions, and enthusiasm gave impetus to my work and your willingness to do the not-so-fun proofread of the final draft is so appreciated. Your attention to detail is impeccable.

To my immediate family, my cheerleaders Braden, Haley, Maren, Jesse, and Keith, thank you for your love and allowing me to freely be who I was created to be and to do what I was created to do. Jesse, you never fail to encourage my speaking and writing. Thank you for taking the time to make me a better speaker and writer. You brought great insight to the content editing process, sharpened my skills, and continually lifted me up in the process. I love you all.

To my husband Rick—I saved the best for last! I couldn't have done it without you! Thank you for your unwavering belief in me and what the Lord has called me to. I could always count on you to say "Yes" when I asked, "Would you read this and tell me what you think?" Your dedication to the Lord and your understanding, support, and encouragement for me to do what I was created to do is appreciated beyond words. Your willingness to sacrifice "us" time so that I could pursue my destiny shows not only your love for me but also for the Lord. You reflect His undying and unconditional love daily, and I love you with all of my heart. Can't wait to see where we go from here!

ABOUT THE AUTHOR

As an artist, teacher, writer, and coach, Deborah Gall seeks to facilitate God's unconditional love and the empowering freedom of Jesus' death and Resurrection. She longs to see others set free to soar as who God created them to be and in what He created them to do. Her message is rooted in her own journey full of twists, turns, and "blender moments," which God used to show her that He is *so much more* than she had ever imagined.

Through her personal path of freedom and discovery, the redemptive power of the Gospel has enabled her to fly freely to discover her God-given identity and destiny. Even her paintings reflect her belief in and experience of the freedom available through Christ, as they speak directly to the heart through the use of light, color, and prophetic imagery. Whether speaking, prophesying, ministering inner healing, coaching, or painting, Deborah's approach is always to bring more of Jesus into the situation. Continually seeking the *so much more* of God, who He created her to be, and what He created her to do, has led Deborah to never be satisfied with status quo. She regularly asks, "What's next Lord?"

That very question has carried her through multiple careers and has given her expertise in business, teaching, speaking, creating visual art, studying, and writing. In 2014, after decades as a professional visual artist, she responded to the Lord's direction to switch from running a full-time art business to founding a full-time art ministry. Deborah's ministry, Abide Studio, is dedicated to helping others find their way to the *so much more* of the Lord and what He has for them.

Deborah's previously published books are *The Color of Embrace*, a coffee-table book, which combines her paintings with poetic verse, and *Heartbeat of God*, a series of devotionals, each illustrated by one of her paintings. To learn more about Deborah, her books, art, ministry, and her speaking schedule, visit her website: **deborahgall.com**.

ABOUT THE COVER ART
"Soaring Into So Much More"

"Soar with Me. Let Me show you **so much more** *of
the places you've been and the places you'll go.
Soar with Me from Earth to Heaven
And from Heaven to Earth—"*
Spoken to the heart.

Seen through new eyes—Heaven's perspective:
A City—the place of commerce with atmospheres ripe to be changed by
the God Carriers.
Cloud Formations—*"Signs of My Presence and Glory"*
"Reminders that I am always with you."
Mountains—of sin and bondage destroyed at Calvary.
Also symbols of the arduous journey of discovery made every day
to reach the highest height.
Wilderness—desert of the soul.
In desperate times of dryness and loneliness,
The Living Word brings sustenance and hope.
Blossoms in the desert, beauty from ashes, joy in the morning.
Shoreline and Sea—mending and launching
Reaping abundant harvest.

From city to mountain, sand to sea—
Ever-evolving times and seasons of life.
Glorious Presence and Living Water ever present.
The wind of His Spirit—the flight plan,
His voice—the guide,
*"Take flight and soar knowing
You were created for* **so much more.**

Looking for

so much more?

ORDER A COPY OF

A Guided Journal to Soaring With God

Keep the Adventure going! Stay connected with Deborah and all things *so much more.*

Visit **www.DeborahGall.com** and follow her on social media for valuable resources.

- Let Deborah be your guide! Add new depth with 12 Chapter Videos including extra content!
- Download a Leadership Guide to help you host your own Created For So Much More group!
- Join Deborah for ongoing video teaching.
- Read Deborah's inspirational blog to keep expanding your so much more.

 **Deborah L Gall**

 **@DeborahLGall**

Made in the USA
Monee, IL
27 June 2021